Reviews

"Will Marshall would shout 'Run Holly! Run!' to his little sister on *Land of the Lost*. Then Will and Holly would race to escape a hissing Sleestak or a ferocious dinosaur. I have loved Kathleen since she was a child and the one thing she's NEVER run from is her truth...no matter how frightening it is. In this heartfelt, brutally honest book, Kathleen lays bare her journey without flinching. Reading this book, I found myself laughing hysterically, and then on the next page, weeping as I discovered the real Holly Marshall's not-so-routine expedition!"

WESLEY EURE

Director, Producer, Actor, Will Marshall on *Land of the Lost*

"What a fun book! A must-read for all fans of *Land of the Lost*. Kathy's bright soul shows through in every word!"

DAVID GERROLD

Author of over 50 books including *The Martian Child*, Winner of the Hugo and Nebula awards, Script-writer for Star Trek, Creator of Sleestaks, gerrold.com

"I read *Run, Holly, Run!* in one sitting! I only took a break midway to send Kathleen a message to tell her how much I loved it. Her story is honest and heartbreaking. Great read."

ERIN MURPHY

Actress, "Tabitha" on *Bewitched*

"*Run, Holly, Run!* is such an honest and entertaining read for anyone. Even if you weren't a follower of *Land of the Lost*, you will love this book! I personally know Kathy and adore her. It's great that others can get a glimpse of her extraordinary journey. What a brave soul. What a survivor."

MOOSIE DRIER

Director and Actor

"Beautifully written and shamelessly honest, Kathleen's *Run, Holly, Run!* is no routine expedition into memoir land, but an over-the-waterfalls plunge into a truly authentic life. That rare tell-all that leaves you feeling like you actually got to know the person by the end of the book. I couldn't put it down.

COREY ROTHERMEL

Host of San Diego Comic-Con's "Saturday Morning Cartoons Happy Hour" and Co-author (with Douglas Neff) of *Epic Win! The Geek's Guide to the Journey from Fan to Creator*

"Straightforward and from the hip, former child star and actress Kathy Coleman reveals the hopes, joys and challenges, ranging from simple to severe, with what it was like growing up as a pubescent performer with a starring role on the original *Land of the Lost* TV series. In the end, it is more than abundantly clear just how 'found' is the beautiful soul named Kathy Coleman."

HERBIE J PILATO

Writer, Producer, Performer, Author, and Entertainment Executive

KATHY COLEMAN

WITH STEVEN THOMPSON AND DAVE SMITHERMAN

Wyatt-MacKenzie Publishing

DEADWOOD, OREGON

Run, Holly, Run!
Kathy Coleman
with Steven Thompson and Dave Smitherman

ISBN: 978-1-942545-60-6
Library of Congress Control Number: 2016951988

COVER: Dinosaur 3D render ©metha | Shutterstock.com
Dinosaur flipbook animation stills by Alex Veresdeni
Photos ©Kathy Coleman.

Wyatt-MacKenzie Publishing
DEADWOOD, OREGON

Wyatt-MacKenzie Publishing, Inc.
www.WyattMacKenzie.com
Contact us: info@wyattmackenzie.com

Dedicated to Marion Dorothy Coleman "Mum"

CONTENTS

Erica Hagen

Kathy Coleman was just a little girl, 12 years old, when we met on the set of *Land of the Lost* in 1974. I was a young actress who had grown up in Kansas, graduated from the University of Kansas, and then moved to New York City. After 3½ harrowing years of living in the city, modeling, taking acting classes, performing off-Broadway and struggling to survive the hard life in the city, I moved to Los Angeles. I was delighted to find flowers on the trees in January, people who smiled and said hello as I walked down the street, and work on television shows as soon as I arrived. Though I did not have a television and had not seen the show, I was thrilled to be cast on *Land of the Lost.*

Kathy Coleman

Kathy and I hit it off immediately. She was not only such a cute little girl in her blond braids and red plaid shirt, she was sweet, down to earth, and fun to be around. Besides enjoying each other's company, we were both amused at the concept that, in this show, we were both supposed to be the same person, together at the same time! "I am you and you are me." The episode was called "Elsewhen." I played Kathy grown up, coming back through a time warp to warn her about danger and to help her overcome her greatest fears. I wore a long, slinky, green dress and appeared out of a cloud of fog from dry ice. Although Kathy was just a child, she was also a very professional actress who knew her lines and played her part well. We had so much fun working together that, at the end of the day, we didn't want our friendship to end there.

It is often the case that, after working together on TV shows or movies, people say to each other, "We must get together," but it seldom happens. However, Kathy and I made it happen. She came and spent a weekend with me at my apartment. We went to the beach and had lunch on the boardwalk. We laughed and played in the sunshine, like two children, freed from all responsibilities of work and school for a couple of days.

Six years later, I had an amazing experience while traveling in Burma that reminded me of Kathy. In 1980, Burma was a country that was isolated by a brutal government and that was almost completely untouched by western influence or material objects. I was in Rangoon at the magnificent Swedagon Pagoda. A dignified older gentleman who spoke lovely English began to tell me about the larger-than-life-size golden Buddha that I was admiring. He had a very long name; he said that I could call him Mr. P. After about an hour of sharing the history and significance of various artifacts, Mr. P asked if I would like to go to his home to meet his wife and children and grandchildren and to have lunch. Of course, I was delighted to be able to visit a Burmese family in their home.

Run, Holly, Run!

The house was happily crowded with Mr. P's family members. I noticed that one of his granddaughters kept staring at me intently. She was about the same age Kathy had been when I first met her, and she wore long, dark braids. She whispered something to her grandfather and he told me, "My granddaughter says she has a picture of you." I said, "Uh, huh," never for a second thinking that it could be true. The girl left the room and returned with a plastic toy that turned out to be a Viewmaster. When one looks into it, it shows 3-D photographs. Looking into the viewer, I was utterly astonished to see a photo of Kathy and me from *Land of the Lost!* There I was in the long, green dress; and there was Kathy in her braids and red plaid shirt! I could not have been more surprised. I had had no idea that "Elsewhen" from *Land of the Lost* had been made into a slide show for Viewmaster. There were no shops in Burma that would have sold a Viewmaster. I learned that this girl's father was a sailor whose ship had docked in New York. He had bought the Viewmaster for his daughter and had happened to get the slides that had photos of Kathy and me. I had happened to meet her grandfather at the Swedagon Pagoda, he had happened to invite me to their home, she had happened to recognize me from the photographs. I was completely stunned at this conglomeration of coincidences. The family, on the other hand, seemed not surprised at all. "We have your picture so it is only natural that you should come to visit us."

Over the years, Kathleen has been wonderful about keeping in touch with me, tracking me down after I returned from two years in Asia. We still feel that connection that we forged when we were both young. Whenever we talk, it is as if we are picking up the conversation from last week. Kathy has grown from a sweet little girl to a lovely grown woman, but it wasn't always easy. This is her story.

Hey there, Readers!
I haven't seen you since I left my successful TV show many years ago. I've been out of the public eye for the most part, until now. However, a lot's happened over the last few decades. First and foremost, I must tell you that as I write this book, there is not a glass of wine nearby. Yeah, I quit drinking a while back and I feel great. The old me is back and better than ever, if I do say so myself.

If you look me up on the Internet, you'll find where it says I left showbiz after *Land of the Lost*, married a millionaire's son and had two kids. Those are facts. Those things actually happened. But they aren't the truth of my story. The truth has a lot more layers to it than simple facts.

My goal with this book is to leave you, the reader, feeling as though we had sat down together and had a long, deep conversation. With a little luck, a lot of laughs, some tears, and an occasional, "Oh my God, you didn't really do that!" maybe I'll be able to get my story out at last, to bridge the gap between what you may think my life was like and what actually happened.

In a way, the whole premise of this book is that we're no different, you and I. We all make good and bad choices, no matter what we do for a living. As I share my story with you, I'll also focus on some of the lessons that I've picked up along the way. The big ones for me have always been truth, love, and money. Now as you probably know, those things can materialize in many different forms, but when I stop to think about events that really affected me, I can usually tie it to one (or more) of those lessons. I hope that my story will help you to understand me a little better; and who knows, reading about my crazy life decisions might even help you in yours. That would be so amazing to me.

So get yourself real comfy because I've got a lot to share with you.

Ready? Here we go!

PART I
FAMILY

C H A P T E R   1

My Debut

$\mathcal{S}$aturday morning, 2:00 a.m. I'm covered in blood and screaming my head off, desperately trying to catch my first breath. It's February 18th, 1962, and I am about to begin my illegitimate life. I was the last one in a litter of 10, the only blonde. My brother Bobby, who was 15 at the time, rode in the taxi with Mum to the hospital. I came home in pink bunny slippers. Mum carried one of those little pink slippers in her many purses over the years until the day she passed.

Everybody we knew had always laughed about the fact that I don't look like any of my brothers or sisters, but the truth of the matter is simply that my mother had me with somebody else. Everyone else knew that but me, mind you. When I finally heard the truth, I was 18 years old.

"It's about time you tell her the truth. She deserves to know!" Those words I could hear my sister Colleen say.

Mum was repeating, "No," a lot. I could hear something like, "You just want to stir up trouble." I'm thinking, what the hell is going on up there, anyway? A few minutes later Colleen came down and got me. She said Mum had something to tell me.

My mother blurted out, "You're not real sisters. You have a different father and he was a drunk. There! Are you happy now?" I'm sure my mouth was hanging wide open as I tried to digest what I had just heard and moreover what had just taken place.

I remember saying, "Yes. Yes, I am happy. I'm happy for you to not have to go on hiding the secret. I only know you and that's all that matters." I didn't have a clue who my father actually was, but I was happy with Mum. It's all I ever knew. Years later we would talk more about who my father was and she even had a picture of him in his army uniform. I looked exactly like him. My brothers and sisters are all from the same herd—the Bucks. Maybe I'm the Buck that stops here.

Mr. Buck had signed my birth certificate but then he was gone. I never met him. My only contact with Mr. Buck was once when I spoke to him on the phone after I was nearly grown up. He called out of the blue one day. I never did know why. He babbled and rambled and I was polite and that was it.

As a kid, I was so desperate to fit in with regular kids because I felt like I was just so abnormal up to that point. I'd go to regular school for a bit, then to school on the set, then I'd pop into regular school for a month, and then go back to work yet again.

Nothing was even keel. Other kids looked upon me as being spoiled but I really wasn't. I was working just as hard as anybody else. Just on a different level. I had to get up at four in the morning. I was always tired. So tired! Had to memorize my lines late into the night and I had to go to school on the set. The travel time also extended the hours of my day.

We lived in a community that was about an hour and a half outside of Hollywood. I was the only actress in the whole town. I used to hate it because kids were mean to me. Thinking back on it these days, I can forgive them because I realize they just didn't understand. Nobody did. There were a few people who embraced it and loved it, but the majority of the kids were against me. I had to be let out of school 10 minutes before anyone else so I wouldn't get harassed. What they didn't realize was that I had grown up in a very poor family. I worked even though I was the baby.

It's my personal belief that my mother did have 10 children. Some of my brothers and sisters would call me a liar on this one because a couple of them were miscarriages. But our mother almost went to term, so I consider that if she went that far, those lost ones are still part of the family. She felt that way, too. It's just a personal thing that I simply want to give her credit for. So my mother did have 10 children but her very first son, Jimmy, died at 10 months.

I call my real mother, "Mum." She had a love for me that was incredible. Everybody that ever knew her has different views on who she was. Some say she was crazy, but maybe that can be chalked up to her epilepsy and some eccentricities. All of us kids grew up knowing her at different stages of her life. To my way of thinking, she really did an amazing job. With no money! Being from Australia, she didn't understand the United States and yet she raised all those kids including two Vietnam veterans and an Annapolis graduate! I have one sister who is so intelligent she's like a savant. Another is such an incredible photographer and a mother of three, while I became a successful performer. What more could you expect out of Mum? And again, she had no money!

Mum came from Melbourne, Australia. Long before I was born, she married a US Marine, which got her to the US in her 20s. She was happy to be here and I'm sure that there was some safety or security here for her, but there were parts of her homeland that she always missed. Just the way that she even spoke. Her terminology was so different from everyone we knew. For instance, she used to say, "I'd rather be sure than certain." Little mix-ups like that were a part of her charm.

When my mother's own mother died, my uncle—my mother's brother—didn't even show for the funeral. He went instead to a baseball game. It hurt my mother very deeply. It showed such disrespect. Who would go to a baseball game as opposed to your own mother's funeral? She never spoke to her brother again. I don't know if she left Australia with that anger, but when she got here, the man that she had married told her, "I don't care if you're Marilyn Monroe. I'm gonna cheat on you." Horrible.

She just didn't know stuff. My mother was very young and naive. I have compassion for a lot of that. She seemed to be just constantly out of place. She'd come onto the set of *Land of the Lost* and then she'd hear, "'Scuse me. Lighting coming through!" or "Cable coming through," etc. She just always managed to be standing in the wrong spot. I think she must have felt that way in life: always in the wrong spot.

I have a beautiful picture of Mum on a dock when she was about 20 years old. She has on a gorgeous skirt with a beautiful little jacket. She looks like a million bucks in that picture. That right there is my image of Mum! Her husband being in the Marines, they went to Germany, and then many other places. They traveled a lot. It was just the luck of the draw that I wound up being born in Massachusetts. She was 41 years old at the time I was born. That was rare in those days.

My mother was funny as all get out, too. She was the most humorous person I've ever met, in fact. So silly, so original, and just all-around adorable. She was a beautiful woman, and as you'll see throughout my story, I had a big-time, complex relationship with her.

People ask, "So what was your relationship like with your mother?" It was … well … kind of strange. What was your relationship with *your* mother, you know? Hopefully yours was a good one, but you know what I mean. It can be very complicated.

Mum's actual name was Marion and when I lost her I got another Marian that raised me another 25 years. Another mother. We'll talk about her later on.

As I say, though, I'm the baby of the family … and I can be a very big baby sometimes. I had to learn to be a fighter to grow up in this family. They're all tough—Vietnam veterans and such, remember? They've seen stuff that I couldn't even imagine. So I got tough. It was a quality I needed in order to survive. I realize that I swear too much, and I know too much in some ways, but these were requirements to get through the whole process of growing up in this family. They all were constantly pestering me. I think it was in a loving way, motivated by wanting to make sure I was all right because I'm the youngest. I hold my own, though. I have to. They used to sing a song to me when I was a kid: "Everyone's going to school but you. Everyone's going to school but you." I fired back, "I'm not old enough to go to school." I'd get so mad! There's such a large gap between me and the next youngest.

One time when I was about 2 or 3 years old, Colleen, who would have been 5 or 6, actually took me to school with her. Then the school called Mum. They said, "Are you missing anybody?" Can you imagine? It may sound cute now, but my mother must have been so embarrassed.

Who is Colleen, you ask? She's my sister. Since I can remember, Colleen and I have been as close as two peas in a pod. We behave like twins, finish each other's sentences, things like that. Even though she wasn't in show business herself, she's been an intricate player in my career. Not only did she accompany me on interviews, she has taken some of the best photos of me. I've had plenty of professional photos taken during my career. And while a photographer named Sean Kenny took most of my headshots and lithos, and was always one of my favorites, Colleen's aren't far behind.

When we were young we were extremely adventurous. Camping was a big part of my childhood. We went on many excursions and almost the entire family would join in. There wasn't much money at the time, but we managed. And I'll tell you, those trips are, to this day, some of my most cherished memories. I believe Colleen and I enjoyed them the most. Another side of our relationship included our love for all the *Tiger Beat* guys of the month. We each had our favorites. Hers was definitely John Travolta. I was more Leif Garret, Shaun Cassidy, and of course David Cassidy. He was the best; maybe a little too old for me, but what the hell?

Anyway, I adore my sister, but sometimes we don't get along. It comes and goes. She can be a stubborn witch (and I say that kindly), but I love her the most. Colleen was president of the *Land of the Lost* Fan Club. She started it when she was 14 years old. Later on, Colleen had two babies who looked extremely similar to mine. Her third baby was a girl and she named her Holly. After me! My older sister, Maureen, called me and said, "Yeah, they named her Holly, but they just picked it out of one of those books by the checkout stands." I got Colleen on the phone and asked her flat out if that was true. She said, "How cruel of her to say that to you! Of course I named her after you."

I have to give credit where credit is due, though. Maureen played a major role in holding the family together. Maureen and I hardly ever hung out when I was a teenager. She helped raise me but she was a real Witchiepoo and for many years she and I did not like each other. Today, like many situations in my past, this has all been forgiven or at least we've come to terms with it.

My brothers are Bobby, Donny, and Kevin. Kevin's the Annapolis grad who designs ships for the US Navy these days. He has a different type of personality from the rest of us. Kevin stayed on the East Coast for most of my early years so I had little contact with him.

Bobby and Donny are my oldest brothers and they're a cast of characters just by themselves! They're the Vietnam veterans. I didn't even know who they were when I was growing up. I didn't really know them until they came back from Vietnam. Bobby and I have become real close. Donny, only sort of. Bobby's extremely intelligent. At 6' 5" he's a very large man, but he's my gentle giant and I love him.

That's what's left of our family—three girls and three boys left on the planet. And everybody in my family's chubby except for me. So my mother used to say, "You want to be fat like the rest of them?" My mother could be very rude at times, right in front of them. Nobody was willing to confess—and they all knew it except for me—that I was different. I was never going to be large. You look all throughout my life and I've never been fat. That's because I don't have the fat gene. I have a different gene.

It was right before she died when Mum finally sent me a photo of my actual father. I look just like him. Same eyes and big smile. His last name was Clark. I should have been Kathleen Clark. He's probably not with us anymore. If he were alive, he'd be about 95 years old, the same age Mum would be. I'm sure he's passed, but who knows? Maybe I have other siblings out there. Still another uncharted territory on my journey.

When I was a little girl, I used to love old ladies' purses. There was something about them that I found irresistible. I could play with them and I'd find, say, an old business card and I'd put it in my purse to make me feel more important. I'd put all this stuff in there. My little trinkets and toys that I played with— anything to make it look like a real purse. That's a very sweet memory for me. I'd lock the purse and snap it back and carry it around like I was special. I had a receipt book with the carbons and I used to play as if I owned a clothing boutique. I would sell my clothes and I would write up receipts. I'd pull things out of my closet and lay them on my bed and I'd say to my pretend customers, *This came from such and such a place*, and I'd write up a receipt and pin it to the coat hanger. I had nobody to play with. It was figure out something or be bored.

Occasionally Colleen would come into my room and bust me. She'd just roll her eyes. Another thing she used to catch me at was singing in front of the big mirror behind the bedroom door while using my jump rope handle as a microphone. "Temptation Eyes," "Sugar, Sugar," "Still the One"—I was doing them with my jump rope. I never would have believed then that a year or two down the line I'd be singing with a real microphone! I think you should just be able to be a kid forever.

Being a kid can be scary, though. I'm guessing it was around 1966 when a very strange event took place. To this day the story still haunts me. I have a fear of toilets, and the movie *Jaws* never helped any because after that movie, I thought there could be a shark anywhere—lakes, swimming pools, toilets. I guess it was those stories I had heard as a child of people owning baby alligators and flushing them down the toilets into the sewer systems in New York. As the tale goes, it was Mum and the rest of us kids in survival mode as usual. At the time, Mum was a waitress/cocktail server at Arthur's Bar and Grill. She was actually a bartender, and although she never drank a lick, she could make any drink you could name. I don't recall the circumstances, but for some reason none of my siblings could watch me during Mum's shift this one time so she had to take me with her to work. I do recall sitting up front at the bar with some friendly lost souls, feeling the gum from underneath the bar, chewing it and listening to some questionable limericks from my newfound babysitters.

Okay, I got sidetracked but back to that particular day I went to work with Mum. From what she told me over the years (and believe me, this story has been told time and time again), apparently Arthur was short on help that day so my mother had her hands full with me, her outspoken 4-year-old, sitting up at the bar. I don't know how many hours went by, but enough for plenty of alcohol consumption and frequent restroom visits from the gentlemen. As I say, Mum was very busy that shift and I vaguely recall seeing the swinging door to the kitchen opening over and over by my mother, tray in arms, loaded to the gills with Arthur's specials of the day.

I've always been fascinated with older people so I remember listening in on many conversations that were probably—well, definitely—never meant for my ears. And boy did I ever catch wind of a good one that day. One of the guys from the bar had just been found dead on the toilet! He just went in to do his business and five minutes later was found dead! So I repeated the story. I couldn't have done more damage with a bullhorn. Under his breath Arthur was hissing at my mother to shut that kid up! Something about eating his specials and someone dead on his toilet just didn't mix.

But the story lived on. I had the luxury of being with my mother alone in her room one day just about a week before she passed. We reminisced over old pictures, trinkets and things that were important to her. And then—not really to my surprise— she brought up Arthur's Bar and Grill. She began the story as usual that she was very busy that day because Arthur was under-staffed and then said, with that *I Love Lucy* look in her eyes, that she thinks she killed the man on Arthur's toilet. She was coming out of the kitchen, swung the door, hit him right between the eyes and he stumbled into the bathroom. It was a confession like no other. So I always think it's going to come full circle. Me and my big mouth will wind up on the toilet in homage to Mum.

CHAPTER 2

That's Show Business

*S*ome of my earliest memories are of children's pageants I was entered in. I'd been Little Miss La Petite, which in the beauty pageant world, is the first category. When you're really tiny, you're La Petite. Then there's Our Little Miss, which is as far as I went. I was only a kid, but I choreographed my own dance and that's how I won Our Little Miss. I choreographed it to *Dancing Machine,* but the damn record would not stop skipping and I just kept a-goin'! That's what impressed the judge and that's why he chose me. That judge, by the way, was Mark Feldman, later a band member of The Strawberry Alarm Clock. "Incense and Peppermints" was their biggest hit. I think it was their only hit and it was actually before he was in the band. As it turns out, Mark Feldman was also actor Cory Feldman's dad.

At age six, I got my first Hollywood agent. You know every kid needs a Hollywood agent. Becoming an actress had nothing to do with anything other than the fact that I was put here on the planet and people said, "Oh, you should get her into show business," to my mother. That's how it transpired. It wasn't like I was a young artist wanting to act. I mean, I had always been a little character, performing all the time and showing off. So I just did it. It was my part of paying the bills. I was the youngest, but everybody was expected to be a contributor. It didn't matter if you were a babysitter, if you ran a lawnmower, or if you were on *Land of the Lost.* That's how we survived.

I like my mother's maiden name, Coleman. That's where my name came from because I was born Kathleen Buck. My first agent said she didn't like that name. My agent said to my mother, "What's *your* maiden name?" and she replied, "Coleman." She said, "Actually I like that. So that's where Kathy Coleman came from. These days I don't really like for my friends to call me Kathy. It's like that belongs in another world. I don't mind using it when I'm working. That name's been very good to me, but none of my friends ever call me Kathy. They call me Kathleen. That's who I am. If you really know me as a person, you know that I'm a Kathleen—not a Kathy.

One hundred casting calls. That's what it took before I landed my first commercial. Can you imagine going through that many interviews for a job? Keep in mind that hundreds of girls auditioned for these opportunities. It's probably even more today. Mum could not understand why casting directors weren't looking for Shirley Temple look-a-likes. (However I did finally manage to book a Shakey's Pizza commercial looking like Goldilocks.) Once Mum got past that phase, the game was on. Grey sweatshirt, blue jeans and braids, that's what they were looking for now. The kid next door. Me. But it wasn't easy.

All of those auditions were painful. I felt so out of place. I had all the same desires as the other kids. I wanted to run around and play, laugh, and explore the waiting room. But Mum had me sit still. God forbid my hair got messed up or my clothes got a wrinkle. I did become very observant. I watched all the other kids and picked up a trick or two that I then put to use during my audition for Kool-Aid. This was a national commercial and my agent prepped me before the job. She told me that the most important thing was to get that Kool-Aid jug in my hands because the camera would be following that jug wherever it was. That would ensure me getting the principle role, which would also raise the dollar amount I was paid. So the pressure was on from all angles, and I was up for the challenge. There were probably about 15 kids on this shoot. The director came into the room and asked if any of us kids knew how to make paper flowers. I was so well trained that I would have raised my hand even if he'd asked if anyone could swallow swords. So up went my hand and the hand of another girl. The director asked both of us to come with him to the carnival-like set. While we were walking I asked the other girl, "What exactly does he mean 'paper flowers'?" She explained to me how to make them so there I was, locked and loaded with information and ready to begin.

When we were directed to stand behind a booth, I noticed that there was only one barstool. In front of that was the infamous jug. Usually before a scene is shot, there are lighting checks, sound checks, and a couple of rehearsals. So when all the rehearsing was going on I let the other girl sit on the stool and hold the jug. But when the director said "Let's shoot one," I told the girl it was my turn to sit on the stool. When the cameras were rolling, there I was on that stool with the death grip on that jug. There was no way in hell I was leaving that set without having accomplished that feat. I would never have lived it down. Like in golf, this was a hole in one. "That's a take. Moving on to the next scene," the director yelled. I couldn't believe it. I could breathe again.

Then there was one for the snack Cheez-It. I remember the funniest thing about shooting that commercial was the parents that were in it. We shot it like 100 times and as the day wore on, they started making comments like, "We fucking hate Cheez-It!" It made us kids laugh so hard because they were swearing and, of course, we weren't allowed to. So they would film us acting like we really loved Cheez-It. Then the adult actors would swear and we'd laugh, which only added to our happy Cheez-It expressions. In fact, in quite a few of the commercials that I did, the adults swore, which made me just laugh and that always helped me "sell" the product.

Arthur Treacher's Fish and Chips was another one. The cast

included a father, mother, brother, and sister. It was very similar to Cheez-It. As a matter of fact, that father had the same crazy personality. He made us laugh through the entire shoot, especially me. I hated fish and every time I had to take a bite (with a smile on my face no less) he would make a funny face at me. The camera angle never saw his expressions, only mine. Keeping a straight face and staying in character was bad enough, and I still had to swallow that fish. Yuck! I thought the fries would be my salvation, but no, they tasted just like the damn fish. Even my soda had that funky smell to it. Thank god for laughter or I'd have never gotten through it.

I ran into a little problem on a commercial for Dairy Queen. Between the audition day and the day of the shoot, I lost my front tooth. Mum was frantic. We had to find a dentist who could make a replacement in three days. A problem we didn't expect was that though the dentist could make me a tooth, he told us that it wouldn't match the rest of them. I remember even on *Land of the Lost* they had to use special lighting at times because my teeth were so white.

There was constant pressure for me to book one of these lucrative gigs. Mum would always say, "You have to get this commercial!" So I'd go in there with all my bells and whistles going and I'd land the job. If I didn't, my unemployment benefits would kick in for another 6 months. We weren't a rich family by any stretch of the imagination. So it was a vicious cycle of either booking jobs or applying for benefits to keep us afloat.

You could see so many movie and TV stars at that unemployment office back then. It was crazy. There was a girl who had been part of *The Mickey Mouse Club*, there was Adam Rich from *Eight Is Enough* (who became a close friend) and, I swear, Cher was there once, too. If you wanted to see celebrities, you just went to the unemployment office. The minimum was about $250 a week—who the heck was gonna turn that down? That's minimum. And that was more than 30 years ago when I was going. All you had to do was one commercial and then in six months you'd be eligible for benefits again. That's how I did it. As my unemployment ran out, my mother would put the pressure on me.

Most commercials averaged between $2,000 to $4,000 when all was said and done. This included the residuals over time. The Formula 409 commercial on the other hand was a gold mine. I was cast as a young teenager who typically made a mess in the kitchen. Off to the rescue was my actress mother, 409 bottle in hand and a great big smile on her face. Standard script. She cleaned the mess while I stood there in amazement. Easy work. We shot it in one day. The average commercial would take two, sometimes even three days. I would never have anticipated this one would be such a money maker. This job totaled $10,000. *Forbes* list, here I come!

There is an unspoken club in the child actor circle. It's almost as if unless you have done a McDonald's commercial, you haven't been in the business. It was the Holy Grail. Finally, I landed one when I was about 15. They had a McDonald's building that was specifically designed for commercials. The entire interior moved around so that cameras could get the shots they needed. Very similar to a show like *The Price is Right*. Everything is on wheels. My particular product was the quarter pounder. My scene consisted of me sitting in a chair in the dining area. It was a close-up shot. All I had to do was bite into the burger and give a thumbs-up expression on my face. I swallowed the first three takes, but after that they gave me a spit bag. Often it's not the actor's fault that the takes aren't acceptable. Some of the time it's just that the camera or sound picked up something that interfered with the scene. I think we wound up shooting 15 to 20 takes. The barf bag came in handy. Now I was officially part of the club. McDonald's fit very nicely into my portfolio.

One of my most memorable commercial shoots was a later one for 7-Up Magic Mountain, done when I was about 16. I was sitting in the front car of the roller coaster with Marc McClure

Run, Holly, Run!

(later Jimmy Olsen in the *Superman* movies). I could turn around and see seated behind me my mother, a cameraman, my teacher, and several makeup and hair people. So then we'd go chug-chug-chug up the hill and then whooooooosh and we'd go around and Marc would start turning such a lovely shade of green. Twenty-five times of me not being able to hold it together! I just could not! The more he looked sick, the more laughter just came pouring out of me. I'm so sorry, Marc. I couldn't help myself. He looked at me and made the barf face, and I burst out laughing every time. It was the Revolution. This was the first roller coaster that reached centrifugal force where you go in a complete 360, upside down, and all that stuff. When we'd go chug-chug-chug, that's when I had to get all the coupons and 7-Up bottle caps, part of the promotion for the commercial. He just had to sit there. The nerve of him. I had all the stuff and I had all the dialogue and every time I turned around, somebody in the back was giving me a look and then he'd get sick and I was like, forget it. Whoooosh! On the way we went. I swear, though, it was a gas and a half. You know how the roller coaster pulls into the place where you then exit it? No, we'd just whip right through that spot, back to chug-chug-chug and there we'd go again. And he kept looking at me like, "You'd better pull this off this time." But the more he pushed me, the more it made me giggle. Don't even look at me! I'm gonna look over here. You look over there. It was one of those things, one of those bizarre moments where you just can't stop laughing.

One of the other finalists up for the part in that particular commercial with Marc had been Charlene Tilton. She later played the young blonde tart on *Dallas*. I see her now and then at these celebrity shows and she is always saying, "I am so glad you got the part instead of me. It would have made me so sick." Instead, while Marc was sick, I was just sitting there laughing. I couldn't help it! It was funny to me!

Mum weathered it all well. She's my Mum. She knew I had

15

all the responsibility. Having raised all those children by herself, she knew about responsibility. Every time I looked back at her I was asking, "Don't give me that look. You know I'm going to laugh." And I couldn't help myself and we'd go around again. Take 17! And there was poor Marc, green. Not only did we go around, but when we went around the loop, my mother was riding in the back with her hands in the air, just enjoying it. It was a real kick in the pants.

One commercial that never did make it on my resume was for Peter Pan peanut butter. This was probably one of the cruelest auditions I've ever gone on. At first this interview was like all the rest. About 100 kids auditioned. Of that 100, five of us were called back for a second look I remember all of us standing in the casting office with the director, the producer, and the casting director. They spoke to us in a very casual manner, just asked kid-friendly questions. Normally, they ended such sessions by saying, "Thank you for coming in, we'll be in touch." This way no one's feelings would be hurt; in this case, they were only choosing four out of the five.

Instead of this kind way of handling the situation, the casting lady stood up and pointed to the other kids and said, "You. You. You, and you stay." Then she pointed at me and said, "You can go." That horrible playground feeling came over me. It felt just like not being chosen for a team at school. I don't think my head could have hung any lower on my way out the door. Out in the waiting room sat Mum with a look on her face that let me know she was going to let this one slide.

All of that work and success didn't come without sacrifice, that's for sure. I was expected to deliver and to do that I had to look the part. My appearance, particularly my weight, was always a topic. Throughout my childhood, my mother had me on this nutty diet. I hated it. So each time she went to the health food store, leaving unguarded all the goodies that were for the rest of the family, I stuffed my face. Everything! Ho-Hos, Ding Dongs, bowls of cereal. I didn't care. If she was gone for an hour, I could put down countless calories and amounts of food. I was starving! Then I'd go into the bathroom. It started out with one finger. I put that finger down my throat and I'd simply puke up everything that I had just eaten within the last half hour. Then, after a while, that wasn't working so … two fingers. Then, after a while, that wasn't working either so … three fingers. Before I knew it, I had my whole hand in my mouth so that I could get rid of the food, because if I got on the scales the next day and I weighed a pound more, I would be grounded. Then it got to all I had to do was just think about that part in the back of my throat and I could throw up. To this day, which is really pathetic, I have to block that thought out of my mind because if I start to think about that place in the back of my mouth I start to feel it. I could be in a restaurant … or on a film set.

To keep me in perfect condition for these commercials, Mum made it her job to groom me to perfection, no matter how much humiliation she bestowed upon me in the process. She made me wear a full set of curlers to school every day. In my second-grade picture they made me stand in the back because my curlers were blocking the other kids. In the third grade, I graduated out of the curlers and into Mum's old pantyhose wrapped into sausage-like curls hanging from either side of my head. As my teenage years approached, the focus became on diet and exercise. If she could have made me do sit-ups in my sleep, she would have. Weight Watchers was one of her brainstorms for me. God, I hated that food!

Acupuncture needles were inserted into my ears at one point to reduce my appetite. My mornings started with my daily weigh-in. Then it was off for a morning jog. This was accomplished by my brother driving next to me in his car to make sure I didn't cheat. I was caught cutting my runs sometimes. Then it was off to school where I could physically rest, but not for long. The second I got home, I was expected to do 100 leg splits on each leg. That was before my two-hour gymnastics class. This was followed by my yummy dinner consisting of Weight Watchers meals.

If I didn't gain any weight, I stayed in her good graces. We all came from the same upbringing, the difference being that my body had a different metabolism. My mother had me on all that diet stuff throughout my childhood, because everybody in my family is large. She kept saying, "You're gonna have one of those lard asses." No. I never was. I never felt like I was meant to be fat. I had an inner knowing that something wasn't right about her fears.

She just did not want me to grow up because that would jeopardize everything.

CHAPTER 3

Kathy's Got Talent!

*I*t was kind of cute. I was about 10 and Colleen was allowed to take me on an audition. Normally it was Mum who took me, but she would get me all uptight whereas, when my sister took me, I was able to relax a little more. So my sister wound up taking me on an interview for a job as a singer with the Mike Curb Congregation and I got a call back. My audition song was "It's a Small World," the classic Disney song. And what do you think? Darn it all, out of 350 girls who auditioned, if I didn't get the part! I was in the band, replacing Patti Cohoon who had gotten a regular role on a TV series called *Apple's Way*.

Mike Curb was absolutely huge in all aspects of the music business many moons ago. He was a record producer, a song-writer, a packager, and then he went into politics and became the Lieutenant Governor of California. There were about 16 members in his group, The Mike Curb Congregation, at any one time. There was a drummer, bass and guitar, and one lead guitar. There were different little groups within the whole group. There was a really handsome blond man and a really beautiful blonde woman, and I was always grouped with them on stage, just because of the blonde thing. The drummer came from a super big drumming family. I was told that one of the kids who had been there before me was magician Harry Blackstone's grandson.

That should really be my theme song. It truly is a small world after all. One of my first performances with the band was at Magic Mountain. In fact, several of my significant show biz moments seem to have been at Magic Mountain. It's just weird that when I was 10 years old, this town, Valencia, California, wasn't even anything—a gas station and a Wendy's and Magic Mountain. Now it's become a metropolis, but back in the old days that's all that there was. I was with the band for two years and went on two national tours. There was another gig at Magic Mountain that would have been my last gig with the group except they couldn't allow me to perform legally because I'd worked all day on *Land of the Lost* and I was only allowed to work so many hours by law. But they had me wear my outfit. Olympic swimmer Mark Spitz was doing the show with the group that day and he pulled me out of the audience. You see, I could be pulled out of the audience and it would be okay and it just happened that I was wearing the same kind of outfit that everybody else had on! Get it? Oops! So I sang with them one final time that day.

While I was with the group I was the youngest member of the band so I tended to get singled out sometimes. You have no idea how many celebrities I performed with on these tours. I barely had my pubic hair and I'm out there screaming "I am woman, hear me roar" with Helen Reddy. At the time, that was the big song on the radio. Once, the group was at the Shubert Theatre off the Avenue of the Stars and I was out there on stage with George Burns, Burt Bacharach and Helen Reddy. We were all holding hands singing a Bacharach song from the movie *Lost Horizon*. I was just a kid and we were all just dancing in that circle holding hands ... but I was being taught by the masters.

So there was George Burns and of course he had his cigar. I couldn't hold that hand because he wasn't about to put his cigar down. But he still made it around the circle. Somehow. And how many people can say they danced with George Burns? He's God! And John Denver was in that movie with him. My agent was the mother of Moosie Drier, one of the friends I grew up with doing commercials. Moosie played John Denver's son in *Oh, God!* Moosie had also been on *Laugh-In*. At one point, he won an award from SAG for doing the most commercials anyone in the business had ever done. His mother would never allow him to take on a regular series because once you take a series on, there's money that gets deducted.

Anyway, who else did I work with? I worked with Danny Thomas at the Tropicana, Burt Bacharach at the Riviera, Andy Williams in Cincinnati, Joel Grey, Ray Stevens ... I did the Bob Hope Stars and Stripes show all over the US! There was only one other child in the band at that time. The rest were all adults, but there was myself and a boy who was two years older than I was. He shoved me off the stage once at the Riviera! He was so mad at me that I had caught him in the bathtub with curlers in his hair. I had taken a picture of him and then ran back into my room. He and his mother—she was one of those weird show biz mothers—ransacked our room to find the camera. Our room looked like a tornado had hit it. My mother had hidden the camera in her underwear. And she had jumbo underwear, trust me. They thought we were going to show the picture to the kids at his school. We would never have done that. That would be cruel. It was just me and Mum having some not-so-innocent fun.

When I was with the Mike Curb Congregation, we never went out of the country, but we traveled a lot inside the US. Today when my boyfriend Mark tries to impress people, he says, "She was in the Mervin's Day Parade!" When he spouted that out the first time, I about died. It was the Macy's Parade in New York City. Then there was Walt Disney World. There was Disneyland already, but when the one in Orlando opened, we opened it with them pretty much. There wasn't Epcot Center and all those later additions back then, just the park itself. We were there at least 30 days and it was a terrific experience!

By the way, did you know there's a whole world beneath theme parks, completely under the ground? People in golf carts, restaurants, seamstresses and all that stuff going on unseen, all under the ground! The entrance to get down there at Walt Disney World is through the Cinderella Castle. I got to go down there. I went to Disneyland one day many years later and I was walking down Main Street when all of a sudden I hear, "M-I-C-K-E-Y..." and it was me! "That's me! Dammit, I swear that's me singing!" In Disneyland! So cool to have your old voice being broadcast like that.

On my first group tour, we had to celebrate Christmas in June at our house because they knew I wouldn't be there for the real thing and Mum was going with me since I was underage. We put up a tree, my family put presents under it and they bought me a puppy. Then my mother got me all this gardening stuff because I have always loved to garden. By the time I came home, though, I had a cornstalk, my garden was fully blossomed and my puppy was a dog! I didn't get to experience the puppy months. Put up a tree, wrap some presents. Ho, ho, ho! That's how we handled it that year.

When I first started in the business, I of course understood that I would make money, but I was young and didn't fully comprehend how it worked. Once I had a few commercials and other gigs under my belt, all of a sudden I had to start looking a different way. The fun things I enjoyed became regimented acts in the search for perfection. These things all started changing because I was more valuable this new way. The tricky part of this was that it flipped back and forth. It could go from, "You're special," to, "Who do you think you are?" If I was going to be making all these changes, then something had to give on the other end. Thinking about this now still makes me sad and angry.

So this is an interesting thing. I don't know if it's the same way now, but back then as long as you were not locked into a series, the parent didn't have to hold aside any money. You could do commercials and they could handle the money how they wanted. You could do a movie and they could take it all. If you got locked into a series, there was an agreement that X amount of money had to be put aside for the child. That's how I eventually got my money. Because I got a series. But all the other money didn't matter to me. I don't hold any regrets at all. Not a one. People say, "I think they took your money." They didn't, I swear. My mother used the money that I contributed to take the whole family on trips. How could I hold a grudge? I wouldn't poison my heart with that.

My family certainly struggled financially. Somebody babysat all one week and contributed $60 to the trip. That $60 was just as important as my $6000. Because that person was working and so was I. That's what it meant. Mum worked a swap meet on Saturdays in her muumuu and it was the cutest thing. She'd go to garage sales during the week and then sell her goods on Saturday and Sunday at swap meets. She would always ask, "Do you have anything that you want to sell?" and one time my brother said he did. "I have a *Playboy* collection," he said. Now Mum always wore muumuus as she got older and it was awfully windy that day. She had about 50 *Playboy* mags out and they were all opening up and flapping in the wind and she kept trying to close them while yelling all the while, "That's filthy! Filthy!" It was so funny seeing her bent over trying to close all those centerfolds. "Filthy, filthy!"

Before the age of 12, I didn't know what it was like to be grounded. I always hung out with Mum anyway. As a matter of fact, I didn't allow her to leave the house without kissing me goodbye. There were times when I chased her car down the street because she had forgotten to kiss me. I had a secret, though. I was still wetting the bed at that point and that's when the groundings began. For every night I wet the bed, I was grounded the following day. As punishment, I was not allowed to leave the house. Grounding me was a new tactic at that point, as her

previous efforts to stop my bed-wetting had not worked. When I
was 8 years old, a neighbor had given Mum a bed-wetting con-
traption he had used on his daughter. It consisted of a mat that
was placed underneath the bed sheet. The mat had a wire that
was connected to an alarm clock. When liquid contacted the
mat, it would set off an electric shock to whoever was lying on
it, which in this case was me. Then, in turn, it would sound an
alarm. For some reason—maybe because I'd worked so hard all
day—I could never hear the alarm. I would just lie there until
Mum or somebody would be so annoyed by the ringing alarm
that they would come in and unplug the mat. This barbaric
method didn't work on the neighbor's daughter either. Maybe I
just had an under-developed bladder.

So I was doing much more acting at this point, but I sure
missed singing and dancing on stage. To come full circle, years
later I bumped into a guy in an airport and he said, "I'm in a
band. I play with Tim McGraw."

I came back with, "Well, I was in a band, once, too. You
would never have heard of it." I told him it was the Mike Curb
Congregation.

"Of course I've heard of that," he said.

I said, "You are the biggest liar I have heard in my life."

But he said, "No. As a matter of fact, Tim is on Curb's label
and so is Faith Hill."

"So you really do know what I'm talking about," I said.
We were just talking, no possible connection between us, and
then ….

Talk about a small world.

PART II
GETTING LOST

CHAPTER 4

Finding Myself in the
Land of the Lost

The Amazing Criswell, immortalized for his association with filmmaker Ed Wood, star of his own 1950s TV show, *Criswell Predicts*, and a frequent guest of Johnny Carson's *The Tonight Show* in the '60s, was one of the first to review *Land of the Lost* in print. In his syndicated column from September 29, 1974, he wrote, "I predict the first smash of the new television year will be Sid and Marty Croft's (sic) *Land of the Lost*, based on Conan Doyle's *Lost World*, over NBC Saturdays starring Wesley Eure who is destined to be the new heartthrob. I predict after the first episode, it will be renewed for three seasons. It will be that successful. Although classified as a 'children's show,' the science fiction flavor will gain adult viewing, too."

Auditioning

The first interview was like any other for me. I never paid too much attention on first calls. I would just go into the casting room, state my name, and give as much personality as possible, although I was very much aware of Mum's presence in the other room. She took every interview very seriously. Mum was more tolerable with regard to me when I was auditioning, so I could get away with things that I normally could not. Sometimes it was the only time that I could cut loose. I'd be able to make a fresh comment or display some type of behavior that normally was not allowed. For example, I wasn't even allowed to say "fart" when I was growing up. My mother said it was crass. Of course as a kid, I knew the swear words, I just wasn't allowed to say them … but I liked them. It wasn't so much that I wanted to be a brat, I just needed a little release from time to time. I watched the other kids get away with murder. Often I couldn't differentiate the parent from the child; the kids were often so bossy and disrespectful. As one of her habits, Mum had no problem spitting on her fingers and styling my hair before it was my turn to read. In interviews I often felt a little powerful, so sometimes I'd say to her very directly, "Don't touch my bangs!" I'd never talk that way to her at any other time, but the casting situation was totally different. Believe me when I say that I was mild compared to a lot of those unruly kids.

As far as the first interview for *Land of the Lost*, Mum thought it would be best for Colleen to take me, knowing that I could relax (and there would be no one spitting in my hair). That way I could be myself. Moosie Drier was there with his mother who ended up acting as my "sub-agent" for a while. She was very successful with Moosie so she must have been doing something right. One thing she did right from the start was instill a few superstitions upon Mum in regard to auditions. The main one was to always wear the same outfit on callbacks that you wore on the initial audition. The other one was to apply Jafra lotion to your cheeks for that outdoor glow. Betty Drier said it was made from the queen of the beehive and referred to it as "magic cream." So when it was time for my audition for *Land of the Lost*, Mum dressed me in a checkered shirt and blue jeans, with my blonde hair in braids and my cheeks greased up as directed. So I basically had the "Holly" look right from the start.

At the time, I was 12 and Moosie and another kid named Phil Paley each had a crush on me, something I didn't realize back then. Both boys were vying for a role on the show, and for my attention. It was like a reunion because I had already worked with

Phil on that Cheez-It commercial. When I saw him I said, "Oh my God! It's Phil!" We laughed and started singing the Cheez-It song. "I like Cheez-It, you like Cheez-It, we like eating Cheez-It! Great cheese taste in every bite. We like eating Cheez-It!"

We looked to Moosie as the true professional in the group. His only problem was that his mother wouldn't "allow" him to get bogged down with a TV series. She focused his career on commercials and feature films. At the last minute, she decided not to let him audition for the part because it would limit his earnings. I still see Moosie around now and he says he wished he could have auditioned. "You were my girl," he says.

So I think it was the second or third callback for the part where I ran into Phil. I had so many callbacks for that role that I was never sure when I ran into someone if they were close to being cast or if new people were coming in. As you can imagine, they didn't give us kids a lot of information about how the process was coming along. If they ask you to come back and audition again, you just do it and wait for the next call, so that's what I did. It was fun to see Phil because we were friends. After the Cheez-It experience, he had started hanging out at my house. Believe me when I tell you that my house was very different from the homes of many of those child actors. Our house was very traditional, comfy, and homey, and not at all pretentious or opulent. However, for some reason, ours became the hangout house for a lot of the acting kids, maybe because we were so informal and relaxed. However, there was one strange thing. I could hardly recognize Mum when the other kids came over to spend the night or stay for the weekend. She was just so cool with them and even encouraged "wild" behavior that she would never allow us to do any other day. "Who is this woman?" I thought. The kids were able to eat "fun" food, stay up late, and even swear. I couldn't believe it. I just tried to blend in and maybe let a swear word slip out here and there. I was never sure when my "real" Mum would return.

It might have been the fourth interview where I met the other *Land of the Lost* castmates. Up to that time it was just reading in front of a few adults and answering questions. So when I finally got to meet other actors who had already been cast on the show, I was excited. I knew that I was closer to getting the role since I was being introduced to everyone. I could finally put faces to the names I had read over and over in my previous auditions—Will and Marshall. There wasn't any awkwardness between us, which sometimes happens when actors are thrown together. I felt an immediate connection with both of them. I have always been such a sponge for kindness, and they showed me nothing but.

The dialogue that I had to recite flowed so much easier with these new faces that I could actually look at, especially since they matched their character descriptions so well. I had imagined over and over what the others would look like and whether they would be nice or not. There are always so many unknowns in the casting process, so I was happy that I had made it this far. For the three previous callbacks I had read with an older woman who was the casting director. If I remember correctly, the fourth audition also included a man named Dennis Steinmetz (who I found out was the director) and two brothers named Sid and Marty Krofft, who of course I knew were the ones in charge.

So after that fourth audition went really well, I just knew I had the role. I could feel the energy on the set. I've always had this intuitive ability to read people, which I attribute to my Aquarian traits, so I was sure I would be Holly. Then I got called back a fifth time, then a sixth and a seventh. I was excited each time, but I couldn't understand what was taking so long. I knew I was Holly, why hadn't they figured it out yet? At each successive meeting there would be another NBC executive or network representative. I was just a kid, so to me they were just nice older men. Of course I smiled sweetly at them, trying to show my "personality" as Mrs. Drier had instructed.

Run, Holly, Run!

During this entire process, which ended up being a total of nine auditions for the role, my mind was working overtime dreaming about the pony I was going to have. After my mother promised that if I booked this series I would have my very own pony, I was a kid on a mission. I didn't care how big I had to smile, how many executives I had to charm, or how many times they wanted me to come back. I just kept my eye on that four-legged prize that would be my very own. Horseback riding had become a large part of my childhood. I also invited other kids to join me when they came to visit. My sister, Maureen, would organize rides for me and my friends at local stables in the area. Sometimes we'd even go on trips to the mountains of Big Bear or Lake Tahoe. I loved hanging out with my friends, but my love for horses grew stronger and stronger with each ride.

And if I got this job, my dream would come true and I'd have a pony of my own.

Getting the Job

There was a show that came on Saturday mornings before *Land of the Lost* called *Run, Joe, Run*. It was about a German shepherd falsely accused of attacking someone. The dog had escaped just before he was going to be euthanized and each episode was about people he encountered as he was chased by a military guy who was trying to save him. I auditioned for a role on one of the episodes of that series. It got down to Kristy McNichol and myself. She wound up getting the part. Had I gotten that episode I would not have gotten *Land of the Lost*. Someone said that Kristy was up for *Land of the Lost,* but she was unavailable because she was already on a project. That would have been *Run, Joe, Run*.

Talk about one of the happiest days in my childhood. After all those callbacks, the phone finally rang with the news I'd been waiting for forever, or so it seemed. Of course it was my agent calling with the offer for the show. "You booked it!" I also heard they had considered Jodie Foster for the role of Holly. It didn't matter to me who else was in the running, I was finally offered the part and of course I accepted. And, as promised, we headed out to the nearest stable we could find. The first place we went did have a Palomino-colored Shetland pony. Very sweet, but a little stubborn. Mum was a shopper and suggested we look at some other places before making any kind of decision. We went to two other stables, and the last ranch had the winner—Comanche, a Welsh pony (which is larger than a Shetland). He was a pony I could grow into, not outgrow right away. Although I did eventually. When I was 14 my feet began to drag on the ground. For two years, Comanche was my best friend, confidante, and playmate. I spent every spare minute with him. He was 14 hands tall, bay in color—which is a burnt sienna—and had a black mane and tail. Very handsome. He was smart and had no problems hanging out with the bigger horses that my friends owned. We would go on long rides all through the surrounding foothills. Back then we could even ride in town and we did. The local 7-11 store had a small hitching post in front of it.

When I first found out that I got the *Land of the Lost* job, I had a wardrobe call right off the bat. The wardrobe lady met Mum and me at a sporting goods/outdoor gear type of store. We picked out my backpack and my canteen. In the clothing section we bought my red-and-white checkered shirt, which was made by Levi's. The pants were Levi's cords and the shoes were "The original Wallabees." The vest was Levi's too.

The first day on set we filmed an episode called "Downstream," which featured an actor named Walker Edmiston as the old miner with a cannon. I remember just listening very carefully to all the instructions I was given by the director. I was told later by David Gerrold (one of the writers) that during the first day on set he was in the control booth and one of my first lines was "I don't want a hairy chest." This was in response to Walker's character telling me that the liquid he was trying to give me would put hair on my chest. Well, the story goes that David heard my voice in the booth and it was so high pitched that it practically deafened him. He was told not to worry, that they'd work on that.

I remember that I really liked the outfit we had picked out. I was bummed when they discovered that they had to change my blue cords to maroon because I kept disappearing from the waist down in front of the Chroma-key wall. Wesley had the same problem with his original blue shirt, so he wound up with a Khaki one. Another thing was all the pampering—people adjusting my mike, smoothing out my clothes, and powdering my face. I was kind of used to this from Mum since she was always pinching, twisting, and spitting in my hair. So no big deal. I was surprised that there were real elements though, like dirt on the ground and water in the pond. I had never experienced dry ice before, either. That was cool.

I was also fascinated by the other actors. They really took this seriously. They transformed before my eyes, especially Walker; but it happened with Spencer, too. He got pretty serious as Rick Marshall, even though it was hard to keep a straight face looking at that nutty hair of his. It made him look half-crazy sometimes, but funny. The days that followed were more of the same. It was a learning experience and every day brought a little something new, just like any other job does.

Filming Schedule

Shooting for *Land of the Lost* began in December of 1973 as we started filming the first season of the show. Mum and I spent long days together during the series, beginning at 4:00 a.m. and ending up back home at around 8:00 p.m. That was partly my fault because I had gotten Comanche when I booked the series and that meant moving farther out to a place that allowed horses. So it took a little longer to get to General Service

Studios where the show was initially filmed, but as far as I was concerned it was totally worth it.

On the set, each day I had three mandatory hours of school and I also had to review a lot of dialogue for that day's scenes. We arrived at the studio at 6:00 a.m. with usually 25 to 30 minutes in make-up, depending on how many little pimples had arrived with me that day. The second I would leave the seat, Phil Paley would take it in preparation for his role as Cha-Ka. If you aren't up to speed on your *Land of the Lost* characters, Cha-Ka is a Pakuni, which is a species of ape-like humanoids. So that meant poor Phil's make-up was of course far more complex than mine. And it smelled. The whole set had its own unique smell, but the make-up room had an odorous combination unique to Phil's costume. The black hairspray for his hands and feet was stinky, but was overpowered by the smellier glue that was used to attach hair to his face. So the accumulation of scents was nothing short of deadly. Phil used to bitch about the Pakuni suit all the time. He didn't complain as much when he had the one with good hair, but on some episodes the hair was falling out, was cut too short, or wasn't fluffy enough. It looked like he was having a bad hair day or something. He always complained about that and I didn't blame him. I liked it when the outfit was long and cool-looking. When it got to that Supercuts look because of the budget or whatever, I could just see that he wanted to have a hissy fit. Luckily, for me, I could escape into my dressing bungalow across the hall away from the smells and the occasional outbursts.

Inside my room was my obligatory red-checkered shirt, and burgundy corduroys and belt hanging on the closet door. Neatly arranged below were my Wallabees and a pair of socks. Depending on the scenes scheduled that day, my reflector necklace might be attached to the coat hanger with my shirt. Once I was dressed, Mum would braid my hair. She never liked the way others did it. If you notice when you watch the show, the braid was pulled more forward toward my face as opposed to being

tucked behind the ear. It wasn't because I have big ears, because I don't, but just a personal preference. And I liked the way she did them except that she was rough, not gentle like the professionals.

Once I was all geared up, if there was time I was whisked off to school. Since Phil and I were the two minors on set, we were required by law to have daily tutoring sessions. The rule of thumb was that whenever there was at least a fifteen-minute window between scenes, we were supposed to be in school. Some days we had to get those three hours in any way we could. Depending on my shooting schedule, there were days when we were able to do all three hours together without having to break them up. As you can imagine, that was a much easier way to concentrate; but it was a luxury that we didn't always have. Sometimes I would finish my schooling before Phil had even started and vice versa. It just depended on that day's schedule. Every week, we got our assignments from the schools that we attended and brought them to the set with us to work on with our tutor. We had the same tutor throughout the series, though periodically there were substitutes, even teachers that I had worked with on other jobs. One or both of us could be in the middle of an assignment and be called to the set. Basically our schedule was eight hours a day, five days a week, with an hour for lunch and breaks when we needed them. We were really treated well by everyone.

Phil and I had a favorite place for lunch and that was McDonald's. Being able to leave the set was a nice break, but it was a bit challenging. First, we had a wired microphone and battery pack that we wore during the day. If we left for lunch, I could take my battery pack off, but had to leave my mic wired. Phil could come out of his suit and head piece, but he couldn't remove the facial hair. He and I both insisted that he be given permission to wash those god-awful smelly hands so that we could eat without out the fumes.

After a long day, the words "That's a wrap!" were music to our ears, especially on Fridays. The work day was fun, but make no mistake, it was work. I couldn't wait until the weekend when I'd get to spend time with my family … and Comanche.

The Soundstages

We had two soundstages. One was interior, one was exterior. There was the pond in one, the cave and the tunnels, and the Sleestak pit was in the other one along with the Chroma-key wall. We had a big bluescreen Chroma-key set that was ahead of its time. Back in the day, they called it Chroma-key blue, but it really is the same as what they call "green screen" these days. I estimate that the thing was about 30 feet tall and I'd guess even 30 feet wide or more. It was set up right behind our little bungalow dressing rooms. At the bottom of it, kind of like how a skateboard ramp is built, it was concave. It wasn't straight and straight again like where two joints would meet. For whatever reason, it was rounded. I have no idea why, really. Nothing was there but a big blue screen and targets: where to look and where to hit your mark by foot. There were cameras set up in fixed locations. They couldn't reconfigure the cameras so there would be this little disk on the floor. It was the same color as the Chroma-key, but it stood up a little more—maybe a 16th of an inch—so I would know exactly where to stand. If you watch me, whenever you know its Chroma-key stuff, I'll stop right on the dime because that's my mark. All those weather and traffic reports that you watch on the news today? It's all green screen. They haven't really come all that far because when I see my local weatherman, he still looks like I did with that little glow around him.

Run, Holly, Run!

Cast and Crew

I'll never forget my co-stars and co-workers. **Spencer Milligan** played my character's father, Rick Marshall, a forest ranger who was plunged into a prehistoric world with his two children. I loved Spencer. I absolutely loved him. Funny. A prankster, a gentleman and a man—a real man. I did not grow up with a father so I just naturally looked to him as a father figure. He treated me like I was his daughter and it was all just very lovely. I was sad that he left the show after the second season, because he was seriously a kick in the pants. He was so funny! He didn't buy into all of this star crap. That's why he didn't sign up for the third season. They were making money off our faces on all the merchandising and we weren't getting a cut of that. Everybody was trying to sell Spencer out and he said, "Ah, kiss my ass," and he just took off. They had offered him another season. Every year we went from scale to double scale to triple scale, and he wanted more money if he was going to keep doing it. They weren't willing to pay him for it and he simply said, "Well then, I'm not willing to be here." Simple as that. That was basically it. How do you like those apples? Spencer wasn't in the business to be a celebrity. He was a true actor. But he was also the one who was really real. That's the only way I can describe him. He was just a genuine human being. No glitz or star stuff. Not an ounce.

He actually even took me out for dinner and bought me gifts when I turned 18. A lovely man, on and off the set at the time. He's completely out of the business now. He's become more of a mountain man and a bit of a recluse. So my make-believe father quit the show. If I couldn't have a real father, couldn't I at least have had my fake father a little longer? At the time, *Land of the Lost* was the number one Saturday morning show on NBC. Spencer had been in negotiation talks, but they couldn't come to an agreement. To this day, even the mention of the failed attempts makes him angry. Spencer does say now, though, that he felt guilty for leaving Wesley and me.

Wesley Eure played my brother, Will Marshall. On the set, in spite of our 11-year age difference, we had a very competitive relationship just as if we were really brother and sister. Who gets the last word on camera? That sort of thing. Wesley was originally billed only by his first name, like Cher. We behaved exactly like brother and sister, only in a show-business-type way. Wesley introduced me to the game of being a camera hog. Here's how the game was played. We'd be following our dialogue line for line and, for instance, he'd say, "Run, Holly, run!" and I'd say, "I'm going as fast as I can!" Well that's all that was written on our script, but somehow Wesley would always come up with an extra ad lib like, "Faster!" Well, dammit, Janet, that wasn't in the script! By the way, this extra line was followed up with a shove-me-into-the-bushes-type maneuver (off-camera, mind you) that would result in him turning to the camera for that last close-up. This became a daily routine for us and it was actually pretty funny seeing if we could outdo each other.

Phil Paley and I had a kind of unique relationship. Some of the people that we were working with at the time may have looked a lot younger, but they were truthfully older. All of them! Phil and I were the only real children, and because of that we had a special bond. We went to our daily three hours of schooling together with the tutor. Then, when it was free time, we'd go play and just run around the studio lot. Phil had a big time crush on me and I used to punch him in the arm. Just goofy kid stuff. I couldn't help myself. But he was a black belt! In fact, he was the youngest 2nd degree black belt in the United States at that time and had appeared on *The Tonight Show* with Chuck Norris. He was Chuck Norris's protégé!

Phil also came from a very wealthy family. He wasn't there for the money. He was just doing it for fun. He and I actually wound up living together for a short while later in life. It was just one of those things that had to happen, I guess. It was never going to be something everlasting, but we felt we had to have that moment together. It was kind of private. We had shared so many things together, why not share that? Whenever we get together these days, we still giggle like crazy.

When I met **Ron Harper**, it was the first and only time in my career that I sat behind the other side of the table. When you go on the interview, there's the director, producer, and casting agent on one side, and you're on the other side. When replacing Spencer, the actors who were auditioning had to read for me! And it had to be what I liked and who did I think would work well with me? It seemed like I made a good choice at the time. More on Ron later.

Actress **Erica Hagen**, in the episode, "Elsewhen," played the future Holly, and it's by far my favorite. She also played my mother in another episode. I didn't stay in touch with Erica after her appearance on the show, but I did get back in contact with her years later. There was a major gap, though, and she had eventually switched gears and begun a whole new career. I don't remember now if she found me or I found her, but we had some good chuckles when we reunited. She was the fantasy older sister I had always wanted. She was really cool to hang out with. People used to say to me, "Are you two sisters?" and I'd answer, "Yes." Her friendship and acceptance just meant the world to me. We did other fun things together like shopping and wholesome, cool stuff that the women in my family weren't interested in. None of them cared much about makeup and feminine, girly ways.

Walker Edmiston was my love! Oh, I loved him so much! What an unbelievable human being. He was just incredible. Funny! A hoot and a half. A scream! Just a phenomenal sense of humor. Walker was a talented voice man a la Mel Blanc, only not as famous. I so enjoyed spending time with him in Atlanta at

Dragon Con. I can't actually capsulize all of the things I would like to say to him, but he was my friend and I puked on him the last time that I saw him. We did an interview and they said, "Was it hot being in that Enik costume?" He replied, "Oh, yeah!" Then they turned and asked me, "What was your relationship like with your mother?" I turned to Walker and said, "What the fuck is up with this, man? How come you get the easy question? 'Wasn't it hot?' All you have to say is yes or no, but then they wanna know about my crazy relationship with my mother! Jiminy Christmas!" He started laughing, but I actually got sick to my stomach … so I puked on him right there in the limousine. They had asked me a question that was too raw and personal.

I have nothing but good things to say about that man, though. We were always comfortable with one another. "It is so much fun talking to you as an adult," I once told him. Back then the adults talked to me but, you know, I was a child. And that was the same with Walker. Of course he talked to me, but I was just a child and he was an older man. He was probably in his 50s back then. Same thing with Sid and me. We were laughing just a few years back about how we can now talk like adults, which is just a gas and a half.

Walker's house was so chockablock full of collectibles. And I'm not talking about somebody who has a curio fetish. You know how with some people you go in their house and there's like a billion ceramic frogs? No, this was stuff from his whole career and all over the world. He even had an airplane hanging from his living room ceiling. His house was incredible. It would take you probably a month to see everything in it. That's how much stuff he had. In fact, he left his daughter with three homes packed with this kind of stuff, so she's set for life. Not to mention his car collection! He must have had 10 cars. All beautiful, gorgeous automobiles!

David Gerrold was a writer on the show and he is also known for his work on *Star Trek*, both the original series and the

animated version that aired around the same time as *Land of the Lost*. At some of the events we both attend, David tells how he got together with Michael Westmore and created the Sleestaks and that it was David who came up with the name. He was the first Story Editor on our show and wrote or co-wrote several of our best episodes: including my personal favorite, "Elsewhen," written with DC Fontana, who also had *Star Trek* connections. I picked that episode to be shown for my appearance at Dragon Con. I guess my second favorite episode would be "The Flying Dutchman," which guest-starred Rex Holman. He was a good actor. He took me (as Holly) on his ship and I was sewing and all that stuff. So much fun.

Other exceptional writers we had included famous names in science-fiction who didn't normally work in television but were, I guess, drawn to our show, people like **Larry Niven**, **Theodore Sturgeon**, **Norman Spinrad**, **Ben Bova**, **Don Glut** and even several more folks with *Star Trek* credits! **Walter Koenig**, who played Ensign Chekhov on *Star Trek*, wrote a script for us. In fact, he wrote the early episode that introduced Enik the Altrusian, another of our more popular episodes. He initially wanted to call the character "Eneg" for Gene (Rodenberry) spelled backward, but decided against it as being too corny.

In one episode, I was dressed up like Martha Washington and Wesley was dressed in an old army uniform. It was a dream sequence. We were in the pylon (which is a gold pyramid-like building with crystals inside) and there was a Frisbee that was thrown out and it actually went back to earth. Then we saw kids playing with it in the grass. I think the visual was for children, but the writers were really creating stuff that would be hard for even adults to understand. We did have some of the top science-fiction writers in the world working there. It may have looked cheesy at times, but it was actually a very smart show. It was really magical.

I liked our directors, too. Unlike the writers, I got to actually work with the directors on a daily basis and they were all really cool: **Bob Lally, Gordon Wiles, Dennis Steinmetz**. I can't believe those guys were really actually willing to work on a children's show. We were so lucky. There's nothing better for an actor than to have a good director. You can produce all you want, but the director is the one who has the "hands on" with you. Bob went on to direct the TV series *The Jeffersons*. Talk about a great sitcom! I talked to Dennis many years later and we had a great lunch together.

If you were on set on any given day, you might see **Mike Westmore**, our makeup man from the famous Westmore family. It was unbelievable that we had the Westmores. Their family has dominated the movie makeup business for years and you can spot their credits on so many of the great movie classics like *Gone with the Wind, Hunchback of Notre Dame, Dr. Jekyll and Mr. Hyde, Blade Runner, Mask,* and on and on!

One of the prop guys, **Max Pittman**, was my buddy. If they couldn't find me on the set, they'd go to Max Pittman. The prop guys had a little room and that's where I would be. If I wasn't in school or running around with Phil, then I was most likely with Max. I just loved him. He was an older guy and he kind of looked like Peter O'Toole. He was a veteran of 1950s shows like *Science Fiction Theatre* and *Sea Hunt.* My mother loved him, too. He was a pipe smoker so my mother would always buy him beautiful pipes as presents. He was a whole handful of giggles. Why would I have *not* hung out with him? I had to be around people who were funny. You can't stay with people who are just constantly professional. Stand here, get this. I mean, even our Stage Manager was a giggle and a half, too, a genuine goofball. He liked to keep everything light and breezy. "You're supposed to stand here. Oh! Sorry! I meant waaaaay over there." And then he'd start giggling. Stuff like that always went on behind the scenes, and I was lucky enough to see it all.

Dinosaurs!

One of the big attractions on the show was of course the dinosaurs. Maybe that's one of the reasons the show has endured so many years. What kid doesn't love dinosaurs? We were one of the first shows to bring those creatures into living rooms around the country every Saturday morning and make them so accessible to kids. When people approach me about the show, it's obvious that the boys really liked that part, and still do! They tell me how cool it was to look up from their cereal bowls to see us being chased by a Tyrannosaurus rex. I love how it made such an impact on people. I think it also helped that we gave each creature its own name and personality, which just added to the appeal. Grumpy was the name of the T-Rex that frequently stressed out our TV family by trying to catch us anytime we dared venture out of the safety of our cave. My character named another dinosaur Dopey; he was an Apatosaurus that was basically harmless and practically the family pet.

The special effects crew actually brought the technology—even the dinos and everything—to the set to help us get familiar with our often invisible co-stars. We were able to hold and examine them up close and personal. Any time there was a close-up shot, they used hand puppets, and I saw the actual full-sized model they used for other shots. **Wah Chang**, a legendary behind-the-scenes guy, was the man who created our dinosaurs. As far as the stop-motion animation though, where they shoot just the tiniest of movements of these models at a time and then project it back at a faster speed to make it look real, Grumpy was the least refined. Remember the scene right at the end of the credits with the ROOOAR? I think they could have done so much better with that. What did you think when you watched it?

Let me tell you a little more about the close-ups on Grumpy and Dopey. Did you know that we could see the glue in the back of Grumpy's throat? Well, it's true. The puppets just weren't anywhere near as sophisticated as the full figures. Dopey was a better puppet than Grumpy, but still a little floppy in the jaw. Since all the Claymation was done at another location, we never really saw that part being filmed; we only saw the rolling video that we used to mark our spots on the Chroma-key, which made it possible for us to react and say our lines. There was one day when two of the figures were on set: Grumpy and Dopey. Phil and I were able to hold them and check them out, though not for long. The man told us how expensive they were and removed them from our possession after just a few minutes. Luckily, my sister was able to film a little of our interaction with a video camera. The footage is dark and a little blurry, but you can still make out the figures and it brings back lots of memories.

Dopey and I shared more scenes together than anyone else. Because I love horseback riding so much, you can only imagine what it was like for me filming the scenes riding Dopey. I can tell you it was more fun than a bag of Cha-Kas. We shot it on the Chroma-key wall. There was a cylinder that was painted the same blue color as the wall and I was hoisted up on it. Even when I had to wait between takes for lighting adjustments or other set preparation, it was fun just sitting there. I also liked the scenes with Dopey's cart. It felt so *Flintstones*-ish, especially with those giant strawberries and carrots, which were made of Styrofoam. On one of those occasions I remember my introduction to jicama, which was used as a prop and someone explained that it was sort of a Mexican turnip, which I enjoy on salads to this day!

Speaking of introductions, it was always refreshing to be working with different dinosaurs, not just the normal four. We had the two-headed creature, the baby T-Rex, and Emily who was Dopey's mother, the brontosaurus. Although we couldn't see them when they were part of a scene, the dialogue was different and the intensity varied.

Run, Holly, Run!

When you're watching the show now, you'll notice that from time to time the three of us looking at one dinosaur from three different perspectives. Somehow we all heard the sounds coming from a different direction and reacted that way so I think it's pretty funny. Even though we rarely saw the dinosaurs during the scenes, we spoke of them so often that they became real on some level, especially for me and my active imagination. If one of the creatures was in danger, it became emotional for me because they had become like family.

Sid and Marty Krofft

Sid and Marty Krofft were, of course, the producers. They had already had several successful Saturday morning TV series starting with *H.R. Pufnstuf,* but *Land of the Lost* was their first serious show and their most ambitious show to date. The Kroffts often came onto the set. They're totally different characters. Marty's business and Sid's artistic. It took the two of them to make a go of it: one to have the creativity and the other to market it. In many ways, our show was a real groundbreaker. That is something I will give to the Kroffts all day long. They came from Greece and they were originally puppeteers. That's how they started. They're brothers, of course, and between the two, boy did they ever come up with some really psychedelic stuff! Do you think someone was smoking something back then? I mean, what did you think when you first heard about those shows? *Lidsville*? Remember when it was called "Lids"? Do you guys agree? "Puffin' Stuff?" Seriously? That flute, and all those walking, talking hats and everything? Since I know you are all curious, recently I asked them about it. Sid and Marty both swear to this day that none of it was drug influenced. Okay, sure. Whatever.

Of course when I filmed the show, I was a kid so I just took their crazy words at face value. In fact, the world of Sid and Marty was smaller to me than one might imagine. I didn't have

45

much of a rapport with them. Basically, I received a dozen roses at the beginning of each season with a card that said, "To our leading lady." It was very nice. As far as daily conversations, they didn't exist. I knew they were in charge, but they were a couple of older guys and I was a kid. A couple of times I did find Marty reading Mum the riot act about something or other. It was usually regarding my lack of readiness with dialogue. Like I told you, he was all business. Other than that, there was the occasional pat or rub on the top of my head and a few "great job" comments thrown in. Spencer and Wesley of course had more of a relationship with them.

I think it's funny sometimes when I get asked about them as if we all sat at the brainstorming table together. People forget that I was just 12 at the time, so anyone over 18 was old to me. But imagine if I had been able to spend that kind of time with them. It would have been pretty awesome.

Paku

Some say that our show was the first to create its own language. It was called Paku and was spoken by the Pakuni tribe. While most of the dialogue was in English, some was spoken in Paku. This was taken very seriously by the executives at NBC who called UCLA's Dean of the College of Letters and Sciences looking for someone to help create a new language. Dr. Victoria Fromkin, chairperson of the Department of Linguistics, was assigned the task. She said that her background in linguistics helped her put structure around the speech she was creating. She decided things like plurals would be formed by adding "ni" not "s" the way it's done in English. Amazing for a kid show, huh?

The Raft Scene

Filming this scene for the opening credits took place in the first or second week of filming, and I do recall showing up one morning and seeing four 6-foot springs in the center of the Chroma-key wall. There were so many strange items on the set that I didn't pay too close attention to what those springs represented. I continued on with my morning schedule. First into makeup, then into wardrobe, and at the same time Mum would do my braids. Then it was off to check in with the teacher. So maybe an hour had gone by since I had first noticed the springs. I came around the corner of my dressing room and there on top of the springs was a yellow rubber raft and a ladder going up to it. Well that sure looks fun, I thought. And lo and behold, about an hour later I was sitting in it with Spencer and Wesley.

Underneath us, which you couldn't see, was a stage manager, a prop guy, and a couple of other stagehands shaking and pulling on the springs to rock us around. Hard to keep a straight face on that one. But I think what happened was that after (by no fault of ours) 15 or so takes we were all getting a little queasy, so it plays to the camera as if we are scared. So in a nutshell, that was pretty much it. The landing scene was shot on our second stage where "High Bluff" (our home) was.

The Only Girl on the Show

There were definitely some perks to being the only girl in the cast. The adults really looked after me, and the crew used to do special things for me. One camera man on the show shared my love for horses. Periodically he would bring me horse tack. Sometimes it was really expensive gifts, like the time he brought me a beautiful new bridle for Comanche. The cast did this double-checking with me, always making sure that I was all right.

Even little Phil Paley would look out for me, a true little gentleman. I remember receiving gifts from many different people: visitors and some of the crew members. Like the makeup men and wardrobe ladies. But pretty much I was just one of the gang. And I preferred it that way. I was a tomboy.

It was a pretty physical show to do—running, falling down, climbing, swimming—but that's okay. Fifteen years of my life I was a gymnast. I'm a swimmer and a horseback rider. Wasn't difficult at all. It did require somebody that could do all that. The difficult part for me was remembering the dialogue. I was exhausted by the end of the day and they'd hand me a script to memorize for the next day. Oh my God! I didn't get home 'til 8:00 or 8:30 and I'd be up until midnight studying my lines. Then I'd get up at 4:00 in the morning! My mother found me many a time snoozing on the toilet. I was so darn tired I'd just fall asleep. It was a lot of dialogue. It may seem easy when you look at the shows, but I had to memorize all of that! And very quickly! Not to mention I had to speak Paku and that didn't come easily. It's one thing to memorize things in English; then try to say, "Sarisa taka!"

Promotions and Public Relations

We had to do a lot of PR and promo stuff for the show. First I did *The Dinah Shore Show*. I was 12 years old at the time. I was asked many questions and I gave honest answers to every single one of them, but then they edited the hell out of my interview. Dinah asked, for instance, when I attended regular school, between work sessions on *Land of the Lost*, if the kids at the school welcome me with open arms. I told her the truth. I said, "No, they beat the heck out of me." That was not what they wanted to hear. Save your truth for another time, I learned.

There was an NBC press party held on the Avenue of the Stars in Century City at the Plaza. It's a gorgeous hotel, right across the street from the Shubert Theatre where I had performed with George Burns, Burt Bacharach, and Helen Reddy just a couple years earlier. The whole place was filled with reporters, celebrities, and all kinds of fun stuff and great food, but I made the fatal mistake of walking out the door and not being able to get back in! Michael Landon brought me back in the first time. Then I did it a few more times for some reason. All kinds of different celebrities found me and I'd say, "I'm supposed to be in there. I really am!" And each said to me, "Come with me, kid." Bob Crane brought me in once, too. Michael Landon (already famous for being on shows like *Bonanza* and *Little House on the Prairie*) and Bob Crane (the star of *Hogan's Heroes*) were so nice and so kind. They both told me they had "all of my shows" on tape. At that time, there wasn't any VHS or Beta even! But they both told me they had tapes of *LOTL* for their children. They had connections and could get copies of any show they wanted, and they had ours! They loved the show. That felt very special.

At another NBC press party, I got to see one of my favorites in person: *Bewitched*'s Elizabeth Montgomery. I had such a crush on her as a little kid. She was just so beautiful. She was standing in a circle of men, smoking and drinking, and I just stood back and watched; I was so fascinated by her. She was such an interesting woman to me. Back then, a cigarette in one hand and a glass of champagne in the other looked cool to me.

For the Macy's Thanksgiving Day Parade of 1974, I flew to New York with my mother and we were staying at the Waldorf, the most beautiful hotel I'd ever been in. I was so excited. I had already prerecorded "Somewhere Over the Rainbow" earlier that week in preparation for my performance and they'd dressed me up like Dorothy. I don't even know why they thought I looked like Dorothy, but they did. They put me in the little blue and white checkered dress.

The morning of the parade, they loaded all of us who were

performing onto a bus so that they could drop us off at the beginning of the parade route. There was a recording group, Bo Donaldson and the Heywoods, out at the time with a big hit record called "Billy Don't Be a Hero." They were sitting toward the back of the bus, all wearing snazzy white disco outfits with red flames on them. It reminded me of my days singing and dancing with Mike Curb.

Mum was beside me holding a cup of coffee when suddenly she threw it over the seat and straight onto the guys with the nice white disco suits! Before anyone could say a word, she went down on the floor. I yelled, "She's having a seizure! Take her teeth out so she doesn't swallow them!" I don't know why that came to mind, but it did. Mum was shaking and convulsing uncontrollably. I quickly twisted her ring off her hand and tried to get everything out of the way so she wouldn't get hurt.

Here I was all dressed up for my performance and all I could think about was Mum. I tried to keep her as comfortable as possible until help arrived. Four guys rushed up and lifted her onto a gurney and slid her into an awaiting ambulance. I hopped off the bus to join her for the ride to the hospital. As she started to come around, she began screaming about my dead brother. She was very confused and I tried my best to calm her down. "Mum, it's me. Kathleen."

I was so scared that day in New York City, but I knew if she were in her right mind she would want me to do what I was there to do. She was always firm about doing the job you promised. So once she was comfortable and they assured me that they would take care of her, I slowly backed out of the ambulance and returned to the bus. I wasn't really in a performance mood after that, but soon I was on national TV singing "Somewhere Over the Rainbow" like nothing had ever happened. My family on the West Coast was watching and later they told me it sounded great. (Of course it did, it was prerecorded!)

What no one realized was that I was an emotional wreck

after what I'd just seen. Somehow I went into autopilot and performed like I had rehearsed, going through the motions, but all the while thinking of Mum lying on the floor, helpless and afraid. After the parade was over and I had done my part, I felt lost. Empty. I wasn't exactly sure where to go or what to do now. Normally, Mum would be by my side, or maybe Colleen, but now I had no one. Somehow, everyone else had gone on their way and here I was alone in this big city. I didn't know where to turn when a hand reached out to me. I looked at the nice man and realized I'd seen him on TV.

"I'm David Hartman. Are you okay?" He was the host of *Good Morning America* for many years, but at that time he was an actor like me, starting a new NBC series that fall called *Lucas Tanner*.

"My Mum is in the hospital and I'm not sure where to go," I told him.

"Where are you staying?"

"The Waldorf-Astoria," I said. I remembered the name of that fancy place.

"Come on, I'll take you there," he said as he smiled at me.

Everybody and everything was very confusing after the parade, but he came to my rescue and he took good care of me. Very sweet man! Anything good you ever heard about him was true! I was only 12, my mother had experienced a horrible medical episode, and I was terrified and alone in New York City with no support.

I needed help and he was there. God bless him.

The Third Season

Right before the third season I was called to come in for a meeting. At the meeting I was told that Spencer would not be returning to the show. That was heartbreaking news. We were a family. "But," one of them said, "we are going to be holding auditions for a replacement. Well, for sort of a replacement. He is actually an uncle—Rick Marshall's brother, Uncle Jack. What we want is for you to come in and read with the actors. It's important that you feel comfortable and have a good rapport with the one we choose."

The auditions to replace Spencer's character began immediately. The writers scrambled to create a storyline that would not leave our loyal fans in a state of confusion (even though in the long run it would do just that). This was when I was asked, for the first time, to sit on the other side of the desk during an audition. I read with all the candidates who were auditioning. It was fun. I loved it, in fact. The director listened to my input. He really cared if I liked the person or not. So when the time came, I had questions in front of me and was ready for candidate number one. All different shapes and sizes came through the door, each very aware that it was important to get comfortable with me real quick. I was very kind to them all. I know what being on that side feels like. But when Ron Harper walked through the door, I knew it was him. He was extremely charming, not too fussy with me, but nice. And he was very handsome.

He had starred on TV in *Garrison's Gorillas* and *Planet of the Apes*, two series that were surprisingly unrelated despite their titles. I had heard that he had also been Marlo Thomas's boyfriend for a while. I had worked with her father, Danny Thomas, when I was a kid, at the Tropicana in Vegas.

After they added the new character to the show, Uncle Jack, it was a little awkward at first. We all missed Spencer and all his crazy, humorous antics. Loyal fans of the show, as expected, were not happy with the switch either. We received a lot of backlash. Fans didn't understand the exchange of characters and the storyline that explained the switch.

However, that year the set was updated and it looked very cool. I thought our cave was especially nice. I just wish Spencer would have been in that cave instead of Ron. We lost a lot of our fan base when Ron joined the show. It confused people. Who is he again? Oh, Uncle Jack? Uncle who? They liked the original "Marshall, Will, and Holly." I really thought Spencer was excellent on the show. We had a real, genuine, and lovely kind of a family bond together. And then Uncle Jack kind of ... well, he just wasn't Spencer and the fans picked up on that. That's the only way I can put it. I think he was looking at it as though it was now *his* show, but Spencer had never viewed it that way at all. It was always *our* show. Ron came in as a kind of Don Juan and nobody wanted to see Don Juan in the *Land of the Lost!* They wanted to see Spencer's goofy hair, dammit! The way Spencer wore his khakis, he wasn't trying to look sexy by any means. The way he stood with the kids, he looked like a dad. But Ron chose to have his outfits all fitted and everything. It's been said that the tension between the two of us is visible in a lot of the episodes; but, you know, I actually really liked him for a long time. I honestly did. I really don't like him very much now, and that's putting it lightly. But we'll get to that.

When Spencer was still on the show, there was one scene where he was dying and I was pleading, "Please don't die!" We were in the cave and I was laying over him. When they finally yelled "Cut!" there were cameramen and grips and electricians and all the crew that were actually tearing up! Give me a scene where I get to cry and I'm on the money. They had to use fake glycerin tears on the others. I never ever had to use those. I can get a quivering lip and make my nose run almost instantly. I've learned that instead of stopping it, it's best to let it run down because it looks so good on camera. That's what happens when you start crying. That's real.

Land of the Lost was the Kroffts' only show to run three seasons. Criswell had predicted that *Land of the Lost* would be #1 and that turned out to be true. In the long run, it got canceled mainly because it started to get expensive. But there were other factors, too. Wesley, for instance, when he signed up for the program, was already an adult. When I signed up, I was 12. I was supposed to be playing his little sister, but by the end I was obviously taller than him. There was a problem there. I was growing. He was already done with growing. It was time to move on.

In Chapter 6, I discuss in depth some of the stories from the set, both good and bad. But before we end this chapter, I want to address all of you out there who have left me dumbfounded with your questions. I think you'll be satisfied finally.

My good friend and co-writer Steven Thompson, or as I like to call him Booksteve, will be handling the next chapter. For the most part I didn't pay much attention to the details. My plate was pretty full with my own responsibilities. Just being a kid was one of them. However, they did keep me busy with memorizing dialogue, blocking scenes, and of course my three hours of school each day. Over the course of many moons, I've been asked questions about the show, and for the most part my memory serves me well. There have been a few of you (yes, I'm talking to you!) who have quizzed me on aspects that I just don't recall. Booksteve is very thorough and probably at one time has received similar questions himself.

NOTES ON
Land of the Lost

Notes written by Steven Thompson with Rene Thompson

Wesley Eure

Wesley Eure was born in Baton Rouge, Louisiana in 1951. Although billed as Wesley Eure on *Days of Our Lives*, the actor, who aspired to teen mag success, chose to be credited simply as "Wesley" originally on *Land of the Lost*. He said it was because no one could ever pronounce his name correctly ("YOUR"). He had been bitten by the showbiz bug after meeting singers Robert Goulet and Carol Lawrence when he was a teenager, serving as their babysitter and later as their driver in Las Vegas and on tour in a musical play. He had been appearing in the American Shakespeare Festival for two years on stage and was fudging his true age by a couple years.

At one point, when David Cassidy was planning on leaving *The Partridge Family* for a solo career, Wesley was reportedly being considered as a replacement; but the show, waning in the ratings anyway, was canceled instead, freeing him to take *Land of the Lost*. The story was reported in newspapers in 1974 and has been repeated by Wesley at shows for years, according to Kathleen. He was to play a neighbor who took over for "Keith Partridge." He did play a rock singer/drummer in an unsold TV pilot starring Kaye Ballard called *The Organic Vegetables*. While *Land of the Lost* was on, he did appear in the teen mags. He was signed to a recording contract by Motown and sang on several third-season episodes of *Land of the Lost*. According to Wesley himself, the *Land of the Lost* theme songs—both the original and season three—were recorded by him and other Motown musicians.

He also became well known as a good game show celebrity with multiple appearances on *Password* and *Match Game*. During

season three of the show, Wesley worked on *Days of Our Lives* with actress Sally Stark while appearing on *Land of the Lost* with her husband, Ron Harper. Wesley went on to appear in the infamous *Toolbox Murders* movie with other familiar TV faces; he hosted a children's game show called *Finders Keepers* on Nickelodeon, become a successful author of children's picture books, and co-created, produced and directed numerous projects including the popular kids' TV show on PBS, *Dragon Tales*.

Spencer Milligan

Spencer Milligan was born in 1937 and did mainly stage work and commercials prior to *Land of the Lost*. He appeared onstage in Woody Allen's *Play It Again, Sam* and later onscreen in Allen's *Sleeper*. He was the associate producer and co-star of a low budget suspense film called *The Photographer*. He later did a memorable turn on *Columbo* as an Irish terrorist, and he taught acting in the 1980s.

Ron Harper

Ron Harper was always a solid character lead as far as his acting, and in fact, starred or co-starred in no fewer than six television series—a mixture of comedies, dramas, and action-adventures—in the 1960s and '70s. They are *87th Precinct, Wendy and Me, the Jean Arthur Show, Garrison's Gorillas, Planet of the Apes*, and *Land of the Lost*. He appeared in episodic roles on many other primetime series as well as several daytime soap operas. Kathleen remembers him talking about dating Marlo Thomas, but that had actually been more than a decade prior to *Land of the Lost*. Marlo's career was just starting out and the romance was heavily covered in all the fan magazines.

NOTES ON
Land of the Lost

Phillip Paley

Phillip Paley was born in Los Angeles in 1963 and grew up in show business, even doing some commercials with Kathleen. He was an accomplished martial artist at an early age and appeared on *The Tonight Show* with Johnny Carson alongside Chuck Norris, then one of the most celebrated karate champions in the US. He went on to get a BA in English after *Land of the Lost* and moved away from show business.

Walker Edmiston

Walker Edmiston hosted various children's programs in and around Los Angeles in the 1950s and 1960s as well as doing voice work for bandleader Spike Jones and animators Walter Lantz and Bob Clampett, including the latter's classic puppet show, *Time for Beany*. He began his own show with puppets he created and voiced that included Lord Kingsley the Lion, Gold Dust Gus, Herman the Squirrel, and Spooky the Dalmatian Dog. He became popular with both children and adults to the point that he made personal appearances at stores, holiday events, and was even Grand Marshal of a rodeo parade. All the while, he was also quite well-known for collecting, showing, and racing cars. His live action acting includes a succession of memorably eccentric roles including the "Chester" character in the well-remembered *Maverick* parody of *Gunsmoke* and a Middle Eastern potentate on *Get Smart*. When the Kroffts began their various TV series, Walker appeared on several, including the title character in *Sigmund and the Sea Monsters*, voicing the role while Billy Barty appeared in the suit. On *Land of the Lost*, Kathleen has said that he actually did wear the Enik suit himself. Edmiston also spent years voicing cookie elf Ernie Keebler in TV commercials, a role also played by actor Parley Baer.

Erica Hagen

Erica Hagen portrayed both Holly's mother and the presumed grown-up version of Holly herself in *Land of the Lost*. The pretty actress played many small but memorable roles in major movies and television shows opposite some of the biggest names in the business throughout the 1970s before leaving show business. She made a lasting impression on young Kathleen and wrote the foreword for this book after the two reunited for the first time in years.

Jon Locke

Six-foot-two Jon Locke (1927-2013) was a character actor known best for his more than 250 roles in westerns from the 1950s through the 1970s. When westerns faded from TV and theaters, he continued working in episodic guest star roles on television. His only two series as a regular were the classic *Highway Patrol* and, nearly 20 years later, *Land of the Lost*, where he played the Sleestak leader in later episodes.

Sharon Baird

Born in Seattle in 1943, Sharon Baird started dancing at age three and won a Little Miss Worthingon contest that took her to Los Angeles when she was seven. Comedian Eddie Cantor put her under a personal contract and her legs were said to be insured for $50,000 with Lloyds of London while she appeared with him on *The Colgate Comedy Hour.* At age 11, Sharon became one of the *Mickey Mouse Club's* original Mouseketeers. As an adult, she worked as a dancing teacher and a secretary before being hired by Sid Krofft for *HR Pufnstuf.* Because of her small stature and dance training, she was a natural inside the puppet suits and after that, the Kroffts used her as a regular on *Sigmund and the Sea Monsters* as Big Daddy Ooze, on *The Bugaloos* as Funky Rat (1970-71), and as Sa on *Land of the Lost.*

NOTES ON
Land of the Lost

Joe Giamalva

Small-statured Joe Giamalva, who played Ta in the first season, worked as an actor mainly on children's programs but was also a legendary stage dancer, tap dancer, and choreographer for a number of Disney productions. In the second season, the role of Ta was taken over by the short but acrobatic James Giussi (under the name Scutter McKay).

Van Charles Snowden

Puppeteer Van Charles Snowden portrayed the Zarn on three episodes of *Land of the Lost*. Snowden had started with the Kroffts portraying the title character in *HR Pufnstuf* (voiced by Lennie Weinrib). He appeared in most of the Krofft productions in one capacity or another. Later, he also performed "Chucky" in the original *Child's Play* as well as The Crypt Keeper on *Tales From the Crypt*. Veteran voice actor Marvin Miller did the voice of the Zarn.

Allan Foshko

Allan Foshko is a name officially associated with *Land of the Lost* as co-creator. Allan was born in Brooklyn in 1934, Allan Foshko worked as a small-time producer, director, promoter, and personal manager. He had been living a Spartan, Zen Buddhist lifestyle, then left Hollywood and became a New York artist specializing in collages. Foshko encountered children's programming while working for cartoon producer Jay Ward in the early '60s, but he left to become talent coordinator for *The Merv Griffin Show* and then Creative Adviser to the Special Projects Division at the 20th Century Fox studio. By the early '70s, he was an agent/business manager to some of the biggest names in Hollywood and began his use of collages in storyboards when he was vice-president of a company specializing in children's programs. (It's unclear but this may or may not have been the Kroffts' com-

pany.) In his book on Sid and Marty, Hal Erickson says that Foshko's credit was simply "a reward for several unspecified creative ideas exchanged between Foshko and Sid Krofft."

THE WRITERS

David Gerrold

David Gerrold (born Jerrold Friedman in Chicago in 1944) famously created the fan favorite *Star Trek* episode, *The Trouble With Tribbles* and, in fact, documented its creation in a book of the same name. He then went on to write *The World of Star Trek*. Along the way, he also became a Hugo Award-winning science fiction author of some renown. He has worked as an actor, including appearing uncredited as a chimp in the feature film, *Battle for the Planet of the Apes,* but remains best known as a sci-fi writer. For TV, he wrote for *Logan's Run, Superboy, Babylon Five, Sliders*, and the revived *Twilight Zone* as well as continuing his relationship with *Star Trek* via scripts for *Star Trek: The Animated Series* (one of which brought back the Tribbles). Although he didn't technically create *Land of the Lost*, his scripts and his work, as story editor and consultant on the series from the beginning, essentially made it what it is and Kathleen has always considered him the show's real creator. In recent years, Gerrold—a popular presence on the Internet for his progressive political stances and LGBTQ activism—has talked about another attempt at reviving the series in some form or other and treating the material much more seriously than did the 2009 film.

Margaret Armen

A prolific TV writer, Margaret Armen was born in 1921 and died in 2003. She penned nine episodes of *The Big Valley* in the 1960s and seemed to have quite an affinity for westerns, unusual

for a female writer at that time. For *Star Trek*, she wrote "The Cloud Minders," "Gamesters of Triskelion," and "The Paradise Syndrome." She also wrote two episodes for the animated *Star Trek* series, "The Ambergris Element" and "The Lorelei Signal." Two episodes of *Land of the Lost* are credited to her: "Tar Pit" and "Dopey."

Ben Bova

Although he has written more than 120 books—science fiction and non-fiction—Ben Bova is perhaps best known as editor of *Analog* magazine in the 1970s and *Omni* magazine in the 1980s. He won six Hugo Awards for Best Professional Editor. At one time, he served as President of the National Space Society and Science Fiction Writers of America. For television, he was Science Consultant for the Canadian sci-fi TV series, *The Starlost*, starring Keir Dullea. On *Land of the Lost*, Bova was the writer of the episode, "The Search."

DC Fontana

DC Fontana (Dorothy Catherine Fontana) was working as a secretary to studio screenwriter Samuel Peeples—himself later an important *Star Trek* writer—when she tried her own hand at writing and sold her first story to her boss. She continued on as a secretary, though, eventually working for Del Reisman, a producer on Gene Roddenberry's TV series, *The Lieutenant*. From there, she became Roddenberry's secretary and assistant when he moved on to *Star Trek*. After having her do rewrites on a couple of *Star Trek* scripts, he promoted her to Story Editor. She continued on with Roddenberry to some of his later projects including the sci-fi pilot, *Genesis II*, as well as the animated Saturday morning *Star Trek*. For *Land of the Lost*, what DC Fontana wrote was "Elsewhen," and that turned out to be Kathleen's favorite episode and a decided fan favorite as well.

NOTES ON
Land of the Lost

Theodore Sturgeon

One of the great science fiction writers of the 20th century, Theodore Sturgeon (1918-1985) wrote the *Land of the Lost* episode, "The Pylon Express" and previously had written two of the most important episodes of *Star Trek*: "Shore Leave" and "Amok Time." The now-iconic Vulcan phrase, "Live long and prosper," came from the latter episode. Sturgeon published short stories, novels, and screenplays/teleplays under his own name as well as under various pen names in six different decades. He even wrote the most well-known Ellery Queen novel, *The Player on the Other Side*, as "Ellery Queen." Cited as an influence on many later sci-fi writers including Ray Bradbury, another of his lasting contributions to pop culture is the oft-misquoted Sturgeon's Law, which states that "ninety percent of everything is crud."

Norman Spinrad

A Hugo and Nebula Award winner (along with many other prizes), Norman Spinrad, although a quite controversial author of the "New Wave" sci-fi movement, has twice served as President of the SFWA (Science Fiction and Fantasy Writers of America). For *Land of the Lost*, he wrote the episode "Tag-Team," in which the Marshalls and Pakuni team up to escape dinosaurs. Early in his career, he had written the classic *Star Trek* episode, "The Doomsday Machine."

Larry Niven

Yet another Hugo Award winning writer associated with *Land of the Lost* is Larry Niven, best known for his *Ringworld* franchise. His first TV work was adapting one of his own short stories into an episode of *Star Trek: The Animated Series*, in 1973. After that, his only actual television writing credits were three of the best episodes of *Land of the Lost*.

NOTES ON
Land of the Lost

Walter Koenig

Walter Koenig was *Star Trek*'s Russian Ensign Chekov. When that series ended its original run, he began a long association with sci-fi fantasy in general, which included writing episodes of *Star Trek*: *The Animated Series* and *Land of the Lost* as well as appearing onscreen in *Babylon 5* and many of the later *Star Trek* continuations, revivals, and fan productions. His writing has actually been quite prolific as well, with a number of books, plays, screenplays, and television scripts all being produced. He remains a popular guest at *Star Trek*-related gatherings and recently brought Kathleen and Wesley up on stage at a Trek Con.

Donald F. Glut

Donald F. Glut became a filmmaker early in his career when he literally produced, directed, and sometimes starred in his own superhero and monster movies made in his backyard and basement in the early 1960s. They became so popular that he attracted genuine actors; in recent years, a double disc DVD set collected them all. He was also a prolific—if often uncredited—writer for comic books and the author of numerous books on dinosaurs and monster movies. His *Land of the Lost* episode, "Blackout," came early in a long line of children's programming episodes written by him, both live-action and animated. In recent years, Don has returned to making his own low budget sci-fi films, often involving dinosaurs.

THE DIRECTORS

Dennis Steinmetz

Dennis Steinmetz would later go on to direct a lot of soap opera episodes, but some of his earliest credits saw him as producer and director on *Land of the Lost*. Of the 11 episodes he

directed, many of them are fan favorites, including "Elsewhen," "Dopey," and "Cha-Ka." He was known as Hollywood's youngest sitcom director when he helmed *Halloween With the New Addams Family* in 1977, a syndicated TV movie reunion of the original series cast that is still shown every year in October.

Bob Lally

Director Bob Lally helmed 11 episodes of *Land of the Lost*. He also worked for the Kroffts on some episodes of *Sigmund and the Sea Monsters* around that same time. Although he did do some major prime-time series, including *The Jeffersons*, his biggest success came in various behind-the-scenes roles on game shows and music specials for television.

SPECIAL EFFECTS

Wah Chang

Born in 1917, Wah Chang was a designer, sculptor, and artist working in Hollywood. His best known creation was perhaps the Pillsbury Doughboy. By the 1960s, he already had a long history working on films as diverse as *The King and I, The Seven Faces of Dr. Lao*, and *The Time Machine* (for which he won an Oscar). On *Star Trek*, it was Chang who brought to life many of the most iconic concepts including Spock's ears, Tribbles, the tricorder, the phaser, and the Enterprise herself! On *Land of the Lost*, it was Chang's special effects wizardry—even on a relatively low budget—that created the often realistic dinosaur effects.

CHAPTER 6

More *Lost*

I remember watching the show on TV in the very beginning, especially the first episode. My whole family gathered in the living room to watch. We were giddy. It's different to watch when you know all the things going on in the background; that's one thing I learned. For instance, the fake trees, the Styrofoam strawberries, things like that. As for seeing myself, I looked at my facial expressions. My face had a lot going on at that age. Big eyes, big teeth. I watched how I stood, where I put my arms, hands, and feet. I was pretty critical for my age. As a family though, we enjoyed it. It really took all of us to make this happen: Maureen driving every day, Colleen studying my lines with me every night, and Mum the ever-watchful eye. We were all proud of ourselves. We did it! Seeing my name pop up on the screen was a rush. I still get a bit of a thrill to this day. It took a lot to make "Kathy Coleman."

As I watched those shows with the family, I was reminded of my experiences behind the scenes, things the audience would never see. Once, Phil and I played a prank on Wesley. Somehow we got wind that Wesley was having a woman come to his dressing room to give him a massage. Phil and I talked the prop master into getting us a ladder. We both climbed up on either side and started peeping through an air vent. Wesley was lying on the table with his shirt off and a sheet covering the rest of his body. There was a beautiful woman really putting the moves on him. He was moaning and groaning. Neither Phil nor I had ever seen a massage being given before so this looked to us pretty damned scandalous! We started joining in on the groaning and then started giggling like a couple of hyenas. It was all going fine until Mum busted us.

Another time it was going to be my first on-camera crying scene. In my mind I was thinking that I would just remember something really sad and hope that the memory would bring some form of tears to my eyes. But what happened right before the scene got started was something far deeper than I ever expected. Wesley walked over to me and pulled me aside. He put his arms around me and just held me. Suddenly this emotional floodgate opened up and came pouring over me like I had never felt before. It was a release of fears I didn't know I had, combined with a loving sense of security I didn't realize I craved so much. Tears welled up from the pit of my soul. Needless to say, the scene I did was terrific. The crew gave me a standing ovation when it was finished. Crying was something I could do with no problem after that. Thank you, Wesley, for being my big brother. It was the age thing. He had known just what I needed.

Our days on the set were pretty normal considering the two unusual soundstages we had. I started in the makeup chair, then moved to blocking, sitting around, going over lines, and just plain old horsing around. Wesley hung out more with the adults. Phil and I would cruise the other studio sets looking for any kind of mischief we could find. That was, of course, after we finished up our mandatory three hours of school each day. During school time, I'm sure the whole cast and crew were happy to get a breather from our childish antics.

In one episode I actually wore a swimsuit. I can tell you exactly what it was, too. It was red and white, like my shirt, but with really tiny checks. That bikini top covered my chest, if you want to call it that, and then I had blue-jean cutoffs for shorts. We were practicing holding our breath, but for the scene it turned out that all we did was dive into the water. On the other sound-stage, there was the spot where we came up, and that was in the cave. I actually liked the swimming part because my hair would get messed up. I'm a good swimmer. I can swim like a fish. However, Phil Paley threw the biggest hissy fit about that little pond because they had put real live fish in it. He was learning how to fish in the scene and when he actually caught the fish, he about went nuts! He just could not believe that he had killed a fish. And then one of the crewmembers took it home and ate it! We couldn't tell him that, though. We told him someone took it home and that it survived. They adopted it and took good care of it. They made a pet out of it. Sorry, Phil. Now you know the truth.

Spencer is so much of an Irishman that his brogue accent was filtered through a variety of characters. One day, we had a guest actor on the set named Ron Masak. Ron played a man who had jumped out of a plane with a parachute and fallen into our world, was stuck in a tree to be precise. Well, I didn't realize that he and Spencer had been long-time buddies from way back when. How cute it was to see Spencer in this light. Clowning around with Ron like they were schoolboys. One would get the other going and from there it was a laugh festival. They really played well off each other, sort of like Laurel and Hardy. On the whole, Spencer was usually pretty laid back on the set. Any day you could find him in his director's chair reading the newspaper. He liked to yak it up with Mum at times, too.

I have fond memories of him sitting in the makeup chair. He made funny faces while he was being fixed up to go on camera. Of course, I was often in the makeup room. I spent a lot of my extra time in there. I liked hanging out with Mike Westmore and loved the little tricks he taught me about makeup. It wasn't any-thing gory, just simple things like how he would sharpen an eye pencil with a knife to get it just right for application. It's amazing what a difference it made not just when it was applied but how it actually looked on camera. I told you none of my family was into makeup and stuff, so this was all new to me.

I also had such a natural connection with Spencer and always felt super comfortable around him. Not only did he perfectly fill the boots of Rick Marshall, but he also filled the shoes of being as much like a real father to me as possible. If I happened to say something like, "You're just like a dad to me," he'd get upset. "I am your dad," he would say and then hug me.

Brooke Bundy was the actress who played the fake woman that Rick Marshall fell in love with in the second season episode titled, "The Zarn." He woke up in the middle of the morning and stumbled out to go find her and that woke us up. As we were filming it, Wesley, who was always trying to make me laugh, had the line, "Holly, get up! Dad's gone." We were then supposed to get up and run out of the cave; but instead he said "Dad's gone!" and then jumped into my sleeping bag and started fake-humping me! It was all in good fun. And my mother was right there!

From time to time we brought guests onto the set, friends of our families. I remember being very excited to show our sets. They were so different and really made the visitors feel as if they had stepped into another world. People walked around half-costumed, half made-up. It was a regular house of freaks. I think it was the second season when I had my rush of Leif Garrett. He and I had conversations on the phone during which he expressed the desire to visit the show. He seriously wanted to come, but the more he talked to me, the more nervous I became and some-how talked him out of it. He made me so damn uneasy. I had met him at a parade one time and again at a Toys for Tots benefit later on. He never did make it on set. We did, however, have a date at Disneyland and shared our first kiss together.

I met Erica Hagen when she was on the show playing the future Holly and then later as my mother in another episode. Maybe it was because of the parts she played on the show, but she really became like family to me. She wasn't better than my real sisters, just different; she made me feel grown-up when I was around her. One day I couldn't believe it when she invited me to hang out with her for the weekend! I was beyond excited.

Mum was okay with letting me spend the weekend, but she did remind me to make sure I went to the bathroom before I went to bed so that I didn't "make a fool of myself." Erica and I had so much fun together that first day. It was probably normal for her to go to the places that she took me, but I felt like I had died and gone to heaven. I just loved hanging out with someone as lovely as her! As it was getting closer to time to go to bed, I started getting very nervous. I could hear Mum's words in my mind so I made sure to go to the bathroom. Erica was making up my bed in the living room. "Goodnight, sweetheart," were her last words to me as I drifted off to sleep.

When I woke up at Erica's house it was about 4:00 a.m., and, once again, I had flooded the bed. I was stuck and scared to absolute death. In a few hours, I was going to have to face the most wonderful woman I had ever met with my ugly, shameful secret. In the morning, Erica opened her bedroom door. There I was sitting on the edge of the mattress with my pee-pee sheets all rolled up in a ball. I was humiliated. But … nothing bad happened. I was instead met with pure kindness and knowing. Erica grabbed those sheets from my hands and slung them aside. She didn't even mind doing that! Somebody in my family might have used a claw or something so they didn't have to actually touch them. I'm not gonna get grounded or spanked? She casually said, "Oh, we don't have time to deal with that. We are going sailing today!" Erica showed me such compassion that day that I seemed to forget that I was a bed wetter and I never wet the bed again! All because somebody didn't make a big deal about it.

That weekend we also enjoyed laying out, naked, sunning ourselves on top of a really fancy hotel. You could do that sort of thing in those days without it becoming a big issue. She was a gorgeous woman. I didn't even know how to be naked. I was so innocent at that age. I was a young girl looking at this voluptuous woman and she was being so cool to me, even taking me out to dinner at fancy restaurants.

Speaking of cool girls, Colleen and I were fans of a new show called *One Day at a Time* and one night, just like most every other teenager, we were watching the show. Mum happened to walk by during the opening credits and said, "Oh, that's the show that you were up for." "What?" we both said. She went on to tell us that my agent had turned down the offer. I had never heard a peep about any of this! Mum said, "You already had a series." This just infuriated me. I was blown away. Wesley was working on two shows at the same time: *LOTL* and *Days of Our Lives*. I couldn't believe it. This would have been a career changer for me, to go from Saturday morning television to prime time.

Valerie Bertinelli, one of the stars of that show, was a few years older than I was, so she wasn't one of the regular girls that I ran into on job interviews and castings. I did, however, meet her that year at a Jerry Lewis Telethon. We were both celebrity guests. A friend of the family brought both me and Colleen to the taping. At the time I didn't know that this family friend had a crush on Valerie. Throughout the telethon, he kept bugging me to introduce him to her. I didn't know her personally, but I managed to get an introduction for all of us. She was very friendly and we all hit it off immediately. She and I exchanged numbers and made plans to get together. Maybe go horseback riding.

Well, horseback riding is exactly what we ended up doing about a month later. Of course my friend would be attending that event. He was ecstatic. The group that did go on that ride had expanded to about ten of us. We went to a stable that rented out horses. We were able to go without a guide, which was the coolest thing. They don't offer that kind of ride often these days.

The stable was in a very beautiful area of Chatsworth, California. Lots of mountains and great trails. Everything went smoothly until we got back to the stable. Horses tend to get barn sour, so they can get antsy and excited when they realize they are headed home. A few of us had already dismounted, but there were some of our friends still on their horses. All of a sudden one of the horses got spooked and it threw the others into a frenzy!

My telethon friend had brought a girl with him who had never ridden before. Her horse was the one that had gotten spooked. In the commotion, she was bucked off the horse and of all places, she landed on the front windshield of Valerie's car. She was not hurt, thank god, but she shattered the windshield. This was Valerie's first car and she adored it. The license plate read "I love EJ." If you remember, there was an episode of her TV show where she and her co-star Mackenzie Phillips did a skit singing, "Don't Go Breaking My Heart." Valerie's character played Elton John and Mackenzie's was Kiki Dee.

In fact, one time my mother was out in the studio parking lot waiting for me to finish work for the day. When I came out, she said, "I just met the strangest person, but he was awfully nice." Okay, Mum, who was it this time? The nice man at the gate? I figured I'd play along. "Who?" I asked. "I don't know what he said his name was," she said smiling. "Something like 'Eldon Don.' He had really weird glasses, but he was so very nice. And British!" Leave it to my Mum to meet one of my heroes and hardly even pay him any attention. The closest I came was when I found out that "Studio 31" in Hollywood, the designer of my outfits for the Mike Curb Congregation, also created outfits for Elton!

So after the horseback ride, we all congregated at my house and talked about the eventful afternoon. My friend even offered to pay for Valerie's windshield, which I thought was very nice. I didn't see Valerie again until a few years later at a Toys for Tots event. She was then driving a Corvette, not the little E.J. Chevy, and she was dating Eddie Van Halen. She had changed, matured, as we all do. The long hair parted down the middle was now an Eddie-inspired shag. I had shown up with my singing teacher who was also a long-haired musician, but he was no Van Halen.

That Third Season

General Service (later renamed Hollywood General) was the name of the studio where we shot the first two seasons of the show. It was located in Hollywood on Santa Monica and Las Palmas. This lot was "old Hollywood." There is a certain smell and feel to an old theatre stage and this lot reminded me of that. We worked on two of the sound stages. Right outside the front door of the first stage were our parking spots designated with hand-painted signs of our names. Because of the distance Mum and I traveled to get to the set, we usually wound up there an hour or so early, depending on traffic on the 101 Freeway. So Mum and I would go to a place called The Steak Shack. This little hut was no bigger than a toolshed, but they made the best bacon-and-egg fried sandwich ever. I believe the shack was there for over 50 years.

After that yummy treat (I still don't understand why Mum let me have something so fattening), we were off to the studio where we were greeted by the same gentleman at the guard station. I don't recall his name, but he always had an encouraging word and a great smile. Lots of people came to visit our sets, but also there were a lot of other shows being filmed there as well (*Green Acres*, *Petticoat Junction*, *The Beverly Hillbillies*, etc.). Behind our lot was Glen Glen Sound, a recording company. If you look at the credits on many shows, you'll see this name pop up frequently, another old Hollywood studio.

Samuel Goldwyn Studio was where the third season was shot. Although this studio was probably as old as General Service, it didn't have the same charm for me and that sentiment applied to the third season as a whole. Yes, our new cave on the set was more modern and our dressing rooms were almost like hotel suites, but for me the combination of newness of the location and the changing dynamics of the cast were foreboding. I didn't know the guard, our parking spots looked like everyone else's, and there were no more fried-egg sandwiches.

And there were other changes at the beginning of the third season. Puberty really kicked in for me. I had grown about eight inches during the hiatus. Holly was now almost taller than Will. That's one of the pitfalls of child actors. Things change. It was obvious to me that this was a difficult season. I was maturing.

After a few months, some of the things that our new cast mate Ron Harper said to me began to make me feel uncomfortable and very awkward. I wasn't sure exactly what was going on, but I knew it didn't feel right. Sometimes Wesley and I would joke around, but we had a history and I was comfortable with him. This was different. One Friday, the wardrobe woman on the show had made arrangements with my mother to allow her to be my guardian that day on set. She was taking me home for the weekend to stay with her young daughters. Unlike my mother (the hawk) on set, this woman watched me more casually. We were shooting the last scene of the day. In that scene, Uncle Jack and I were sitting in the cave listening to Will play the guitar. I was sitting innocently on the floor, leaning between Uncle Jack's legs, smiling at Will as I had been directed to do. All of a sudden, I feel Uncle Jack rubbing his crotch into my lower back right above my butt. I freaked out and so did the women in the show's control booth who were watching the filming (it was all caught on tape). We found out soon enough that Ron had apparently been making inappropriate advances toward them as well.

Everything went crazy for a minute and then became very quiet. I was whisked off to my chaperone's house for the weekend as planned and nobody discussed what had just happened. It felt like it was just some freak dream. Everything was as normal as possible over the course of the weekend as I visited with her girls, but on Monday morning, the freak dream turned out to be as real as a heart attack. I don't know who told my mother what had happened on Friday, but she was on set and she was livid! Can you imagine that situation? Some executives were on hand as well, trying desperately to calm my raging mother. I could hear her screaming, "How could you let this happen to my daughter? Why didn't someone call me? Did you think this would just go away and get swept under one of your fancy rugs?" She was screaming so loud it was deafening to me.

Eventually, after the dust settled, my mother was presented with two options. If she were to report this event, the show would be shut down. She was asked if instead she (and I) would take an apology from Ron. I had to watch my mother make this extremely difficult decision. We were not a wealthy family by any means. My job was very important to our survival. My heart breaks just remembering this moment. I had to watch my mother make this no-win decision. I knew her so well. Her pride and her love for me was being challenged to the core of her being. I wish she had had the ability to say, "Kiss my ass. I do not care if you close the set down!" But because my money paid rent on our home, she had to bite it and accept the so-called apology.

So I stood there with her and we waited for him to come out and apologize and when he did, you know what he said to me? He said, "I'm sorry that you thought something happened to you." What? That apology was damaging to my 14-year-old mind. The shame and embarrassment haunted me for years and certainly affected my self-esteem. It all came down to one thing: money. It was about power, too, but that often tagged along with the money issue. They were usually intertwined for me. I would deal with that throughout my life.

Why wasn't the show shut down immediately? It would have been for any other little girl. There had been a price put on my head and my mother felt she had to accept it. Right there and then I knew exactly what I was worth. Something for everyone else, but fucked up crumbs for me. A lot of "she's fine" and "she'll be okay" phrases were thrown around. What exactly is "fine"?

Any taped evidence has long since been destroyed.

PART III
LIFE AFTER
LOST

CHAPTER 7

Looking Back and Moving On

*T*he end of the show was a real shocker, only the shocking part didn't come immediately. It had a delayed reaction. Maybe a couple of weeks went by where I enjoyed the time off. Then I realized that such a level of attention wasn't easy to replace. "Clean your room." "Take out the trash." "Feed the dog." Those were the directions I was now getting. Of course there's nothing wrong with that as long as you've never known anything different.

An aspect of being part of a cast that had taken a little getting used to during the show was receiving all the gifts you are given as a celebrity. People were always bringing what I'd refer to as "prizes" when they came to the set. I had always worked for things that I wanted, but all of this extreme attention is something you can get accustomed to very quickly; now that was gone. Also, being part of a series is one of the hardest places to leave emotionally. You know when you spill a drink and you see the original dollop but then it finds a skinnier path and begins to travel away? That's what it felt like to me. The attention slowly finds a path away from you and you start hearing a lot of words like "was, has, used to, back then, remember …" I discovered that I had to leave some other things behind on the coat hanger along with that red-checkered shirt.

Sometimes in this industry, it can be just a matter of who you know at just the right time. One night I was out to dinner with Erica Hagen and a television producer who was a friend of hers. We were at a famous restaurant across from Burbank studios. That studio at the time was where a lot of the primetime drama series were shot, one of those being *Adam-12*. As it turns out, Erica's friend happened to be a producer of that show and over dinner Erica said to him, "We needed to find this girl some work." Simple as that. He said he had the perfect part!

Adam-12 was about a typical day in the life of two police officers, played by Martin Milner and Kent McCord. However, in the episode that I did, Martin Milner's character was filling in at a desk job for some reason, and his replacement on the streets was a very young and cute Mark Harmon (*NCIS*). I only had about a 90-second shot, three or four lines. Somebody had stolen my mother's purse and I had to give the officers my description of the perp (police talk). It was a fun day's shoot and quite a bit different from the work I did on *Land of the Lost*. I'm pretty sure this was one of Mark Harmon's first acting jobs.

Despite a few parts here and there, the roles were hard to come by and the money started to tighten up. Bye-bye *Land of the Lost*, hello high school. My clothes were not so good since I never had any spending money of my own. Mum never let me. She was afraid I'd buy food at school, gain weight, and never work again. Now keep in mind I was with kids who knew I'd been in the business and just assumed I was rich. Well, I wasn't at all. So when you don't have the clothes and the cash to hang out with the other rich kids, you tend to stray towards the kids who are prone to trouble. So I gave that a try. Didn't quite fit into that group. Mum was way too strict to let that get too far out of hand. But I really tried. Then I tried the loner role. My self-esteem was at an all-time low. I was a fish out of water. I belonged nowhere.

I recall that the occasional Linda Blair "Movie of the Week" made a real impression on me. She was an actress often playing the role of a girl who had to struggle through life and that was what was happening to me in real life. So I could relate to the characters as well as Linda Blair the actress. Except for one thing. She was working and being appreciated. I was flopping. I couldn't seem to get back into the fish bowl no matter how hard I tried. I was 16 and there wasn't a lot of work out there for girls my age when they could hire a young-looking 18-year-old for a part and avoid child welfare workers and the three-hour-a-day schooling required by law.

I started to feel like I had no other choice but to try and fit in with my peers. I was by then attending regular school with Friday night football games and Saturday night parties. Prior to this period, the parties I went to were catered, and limousines were my mode of transportation. Now it became beers, used bongs, and if I give you a couple of bucks for gas can I get a ride to the party? As hard as I tried, though, I never really seemed to fit in. Kids my age thought about different things than I did. I was used to being around adults and having adult responsibilities. My mother used to regulate who I could hang out with and I had a lot more freedom if the company I was keeping came from within the industry. As the jobs became fewer and farther between, I saw less of my industry friends and more of the kids that lived on the block. Mum tried her darndest to keep a tight rein on me, but I was between two worlds and if I couldn't learn to mingle into the real one I was going to be one lonely camper.

I did get a slight boost of confidence when I was 17 years old and I got chosen for a Burger King commercial. They could have picked anybody but they picked me, which was kind of cool. It really truly is unheard of. We went in as groups of four. They took three girls out of one group and pulled me out of another group and put me in with them. I was the only one on that set that still had to have a teacher and a welfare worker. It was a series of Burger King ads where we got to sing. It was fun but short-lived.

Dichotomy. This one word describes my life to a T. I was in the back of a limousine one minute and on a twenty-five cent bus ride the next. I'm not sure if accepting a life that flowed this way has been purely survival instincts I've developed from a young age, or is an art form honed over the years. I just know this is how I operate through life. The art form I speak of can be described as weaving some of my earliest memories of being in this industry into a personality resulting from my profession.

Auditions: this process in itself sets you up for one wild, emotional ride. As a child you do not have a resume, a home, bank statements, or other means to define yourself to the outside world. Five minutes is pretty much it. In this five-minute period of time, you have to win the hearts of very complicated and confused grown-up versions of yourself. Casting people have been known to be unsuccessful actors. Try to figure that mess out.

Even if you could have adult logic, in this window of time you need to slip very quickly into your emotional tap shoes, scan the room for the most compassionate being, and try to make a memorable impression on them that will have your agent's phone ringing within the next 24 hours. Because, god forbid if you don't. It's not that life will end; no, not that; something way frickin' worse.

Those other adult faces you have to look into, the groups: the disappointed or the questioners (I hated this one). "Well, what did you (or they) say?" The people who ask the questions became my private enemies. What did they expect in five minutes? Well, let's see: I told them my name, I was smiling, yes, and I skipped and pointed my toes all the way out the door, okay?

So over the course of my life I've fine-tuned this process, knowing full well how precious time is. I've developed and mastered the art of quickly bringing people into my fold. Within a very short amount of time I can get very close to people, cut to the chase, and get through the bull. And this is genuine, believe

it or not. Although it does come with a few side effects. It can be very draining and at times I need to make a break for the nearest outlet to plug myself into.

That limousine/bus paradox that I mentioned earlier all stems from never really knowing who the hell I am. I recall different occasions as a child when I behaved at home as I was taught to do in the public eye. And was asked, "Who the heck do you think you are?" Oh now, that's a great question. Let's see, do you want to start with what my real name is or do you want to skip to the good stuff?

Now I find that sometimes I run to the character of Holly Marshall for protection. You see, she represents all of the faces of the groups. The nightmare questioners. Holly is celluloid proof that I said and did the right thing because the agent's phone rang.

Dichotomy. I feel like I'm always brushing the tears off my smile.

CHAPTER 8

Cars and Boys

I once had a Toyota Tercel. I really like Toyotas because you can just drive them into the ground. My Tercel's name was Lalalala. You have to give your cars names because when they start to give you problems, like going up a hill, you have to call it by name, "C'mon Lalalala, you can do it!" and I swear I'd always get to the top of that damn hill. My other one was Bob, after Marley. "Come on, Bob! You can do it!"

My mother used to have a car that actually seemed to miss her. She'd park it on a driveway or in the parking lot of a grocery store or something, and he'd start honking all by himself! The Beige Bomber. We had Frank the Tank, our old Plymouth Fury, and the Beige Bomber. We had songs and everything for the cars.

In spite of the abuse heaped on me at school, I had a best friend, and she had a brother who was on the football team. Let me tell you, he was the cat's meow around school. I used to spend the night at her house all the time and one night, one thing led to another and I finally wound up with him. He may have been a big jock on campus, but to me, he was the worst. Talk about wrecking a girl's dream of what the first time was supposed to be like! In retrospect, it was just so gross. He might as well have just hit me in the head with his football helmet! It was just … horrible.

My second experience would end up being what I consider in my mind to be my first. It was the first day my mother let me drive Frank the Tank to school. I was 16 years old and going to high school and she finally trusted me to take Frank the Tank. He was tilted up in the front and leaned to one side and he was this godforsaken gold color; he was hideous, but I was driving him. That first day that I got to take him to school, I was going up the road and, damn it all, if Frank didn't decide to take a shitter in the middle of the road. I was at a light and there were two lanes going straight and a left turn lane on the side of me. I was in the middle one. There was a gas station in front of me. I was panicking because I knew Mum was going to somehow blame it on me that I must have broken Frank. I was in a total panic. So I got out, made sure I locked him up and everything because God forbid anybody should steal him. I went running into the gas station and said that I needed some help. "Can somebody help me get my tank off the road while I call my mother?" Just then the most gorgeous guy came out of the gas station to help. Now I'm very finicky when I say gorgeous. This was a truly beautiful guy and he got my car into the gas station.

He said, "You know what? I'm gonna drop you off at school, I'm gonna work on the car, and then I will be there at 3 o'clock to pick you up."

I said, "I can't give you my car. Mum will kill me!"

"No, trust me. I will be there to pick you up."

"You'd better not be lying to me! I'd be grounded for life!"

He did drop me off at school, but all that day I couldn't concentrate on anything. Who was the leader of the Huns in 453 AD? "Uh … Frank the Tank?" Okay, it was Attila the Hun, but I couldn't focus on anything else. I finally got out of school and I was looking around like a mad dog and there he was and there's Frank running in perfect condition! Never once charged me a nickel or anything. But he said he'd like to take me on a date … and we went out. That is when I really, truly lost my virginity. And I lost it with a beautiful, beautiful spirit, inside and out. He was so gentle with me. I thought, "So this is what making love is! Alrighty then!" Mum never was the wiser about Frank the Tank. It was her car, but she never knew he'd had a nervous breakdown in the middle of the road that day. However, my life would never be the same after I opened my big mouth.

"Are *you* a virgin?" Do you remember when this question plagued your life? In junior high, I remember looking at the girls that I knew weren't virgins. They seemed to carry a knowing or a secret. When this question was being asked, I of course was a virgin. I was a skinny, undeveloped one at that, which made it all the worse in my mind. Up until the eighth grade, I'd never even made out with anyone. Sure I kissed plenty of people, but never the tongue watusi. I didn't spend enough time in regular school to buckle under the peer pressure. Thank god I had my few friends who were also virgins. These were the girls who were into riding their horses, not impressing the boys.

Over the eighth grade summer, things started to change. Of the four girlfriends I had, I was the first to get my period. I recall shopping for school clothes that summer and being surprised that the jeans I was trying on now had the signs of hips. My straight-as-a-board gymnastics body was taking on a new shape. My "A" cup bra was even a little snug. I hated the way "periods" were talked about in my family. I was determined to handle mine differently. Maureen used to call it her "friend." Gross! I refused to wear pads and I was prepared to mentally block out cramps. The funny thing is I never got them.

I really just didn't want to make it into a big ordeal. And for the most part it wasn't. Of course all the boys now were affected by the pheromones flying around the schoolyard. I even received glances I'd not been given in the past. Here is where it gets weird for me. From Dinah Shore on down the line, people have always assumed that I was popular in school. Well, I was cute and sweet and probably should have been in the big picture, but I wasn't; not at all. Sure everyone knew who I was. The freak on

LOTL, but that didn't gain me any brownie points. Just the opposite.

Not only was I a virgin, but I was also the only kid in show business in this little town. I've mentioned how money had affected my life (and there's more to come), but there's another area where my troubles seem to stem from. All of it being on a sexual level. Colleen and I were thick as thieves, at least I always believed we were. However, I had broken an unspoken rule. Partners in crime together, but I committed a crime outside of our relationship.

When I finally did lose my virginity, this I did alone; well, at least without her. Not only did I do something without her, but I kept it from her. The fact that I was three years younger didn't help matters either. She was still a virgin. The way she found out about me was not good. A friend of ours let the cat out of the bag. This friend just assumed Colleen knew. She thought Colleen knew everything that I had done. I now had that look of knowing and having a secret. Finding out the way she did caused not only Colleen to come unglued, but Mum and Maureen as well. I didn't expect Maureen to understand; that was a given. I knew Mum would be angry, but not the magnitude of hurt she expressed. And then there was Colleen. Her anger and hurt feelings surpassed Mum's by a longshot. In the Amish communities people are shunned for inappropriate behaviors. Well, that's exactly what happened to me.

Colleen went home and told our mother and I went on the run! They came after me in the damn mall of all places, calling me a whore in front of many, many people. "Now that you've ruined yourself …" they said. I ran for what seemed like miles in the rain. I ran and ran and ran and I wound up in a phone booth. I called a friend who called my sister. I was told to stay in the phone booth and Colleen would come get me. When she picked me up and we arrived back home, they were all packing my stuff—moving me out! Maureen and Colleen, my own two sisters and my mother, were moving me out of my own room! They were going to ship me to Baltimore to live with my brother. It was craziness. It was horrible. My mother came into my room. I was just sitting there. She said, "I don't want you to go," and I pleaded, "Well, I don't wanna go!" Then my mother left and my sister came in and said, "If you don't leave, I will make life hell for you. How could you do this to me?"

I ran across the street to the supermarket and I called my brother, Bobby, in Simi Valley, and I told him they had the plane ticket. Yes, my mother had gone as far as buying me a plane ticket. They were handing it to me to make me go away. My sisters were packing all my stuff. He just said, "Bullshit. I'm coming to get you." And that's just what happened. It was all so weird. Bobby was living back in that town that I felt hated me, but I went to live with him because I wasn't allowed to stay with Mum. Nobody in the house where my mother and my sisters lived would even talk to me. It took my sister a year to apologize.

So I went to work at 16. I worked once a week at a swap meet selling produce. I got good grades in school. I got an A in American Government. That's pretty good. I was taking two electives: ceramic pottery and weightlifting. I never graduated high school, though, and I'll tell you why. My birthday's in February. My mother had already purchased a beautiful ring that she was going to give me as a graduation present. But I got my trust fund, my money from my work, when I turned 18 that February. Turned out to be a good thing and a bad thing. After what seemed like a lifetime, adulthood was here and so was my trust fund. Freedom! You couldn't get any cooler than I thought I was. All the control of my family was behind me. I was free and loving every single glorious second of it. At the time, my brother worked for the largest Ford dealership around and I got a brand-new custom Mustang. What a beautiful car! I drove everywhere blasting Blondie's "Call Me" on my fancy car stereo, shades on, blonde hair whipping in the wind. Life was suddenly wonderful.

I also bought new clothes and took the family on a trip to Hawaii since we had cautiously reconciled after the whole virginity fiasco. Unfortunately, the trip backfired. Even though it was on my dime, it felt as though Mum and Maureen were doling out the itinerary. It became all about control once again. So in order to have the trip I wanted, we had to have a big blowout and spent the entire trip separated into two groups—Colleen and I on one side of the island and Mum and Maureen on the other. Never saw them the whole trip.

If you haven't spotted the pattern, let me point it out for you. Money, money, money. Sure, there have been other issues in my life, big ones; but money seems to always be looming in the forefront. First I was making lots of money for the family, then not enough, and then got my trust fund and blew through it all—and even part of that was spent on the family.

I guess it's understandable that people think all celebrities are rich. The way we are showcased on TV is pretty convincing. When I was growing up the kids at school used to say, "It must be nice being a millionaire." Not only was I not a millionaire, but the truth was that I never knew how much money I made, nor did I care. I had a full stomach and so did my pony. We had plenty of family outings and we all had fairly nice clothes to wear. Most people won't understand the words "SAG scale," but it's basically the minimum that an actor can be paid based on the type of role, as set by the union. That is exactly what I earned on *Land of the Lost*: SAG scale the first year. Double SAG scale second season and triple the third. No millionaire here. Residuals were non-existent. The majority of Saturday morning shows were cartoons, not live action like ours.

I was, however, very much aware of the importance of my job and the contribution I made to the family. There were gradual improvements in our lifestyle, which befitted us all. "This new couch is comfy." It's weird, after I wrote that last line I started crying and I'm trying to evaluate why. All I could come up with was back then money represented simple things. Now, money has twisted its way through all the lessons I had to learn about relationships, my self-value and what it is I actually like about money. The controlling aspect of money has proven to be poison to my soul. I have had to learn not to let anyone take me out of my rhythm. In doing that I've become very rich in my self-investment.

Even in my relationship today, my boyfriend tells me, "If you want to control your own life you're going to have to make your own money." Well of course that makes sense, right? Wait a minute, I have made my own money, and I don't recall having ever had much control. You know, I just don't get it. For the most part I trust in the universe. I always seem to have just what I need. I'm very generous and I don't, as far as I know, try to block the flow of money. Money issues, I thought, seemed to happen with cheap, selfish people who try and hold on to it too tightly.

Maybe money scares me.

CHAPTER 9

Alarm Bells

*H*ave you ever heard of Robert Bell? No? Well, neither had I at that point, but every police department in Southern California knew whether he wore boxers or briefs. Mum and I had one funny thing in common: we weren't attracted to redheads. Bob proved to be the exception, at least at first. He was a regular carrot top. When I met him, he was mellow, super calm and serene. He filled his days by playing guitar and smoking pot. His jean pant legs were held together by safety pins. By looking at him, you would never think this guy had two nickels in his pocket, let alone a two-page rap sheet. What can I say? I totally couldn't resist him.

When I met Bob, he was living at a communal house. It was a modest little residence that I nicknamed the Noble House. This place was home to a good 20 people on any given day: plenty of characters, consisting of rich kids, homeless folks, bikers, a model, a karate guy, etc. I had been dating a guy at the time and we ended up there, but one night my boyfriend was abusive to me and Bob, like a rabid dog, defended me and took him out! That's when he and I became an item. I found out later that Bob actually owned the Noble House.

A few months into our relationship, he took me out to meet his parents on their ranch in Ojai, California. Holy Mother of God! This place was insanely beautiful. The family members, it turned out, were the original founders of Bel-Air. In comparison, my trust fund suddenly looked like a piggy bank. These people were as wealthy as the Hiltons. Until that Ojai trip, I thought I was the only one of us with any money.

Everyone in Bob's family seemed to like me, until they found out I was pregnant. It was a surprise for all of us. Bob and I weren't sure what to do, but we thought telling everyone was best so that it was all out in the open. Big mistake. Overnight, they started treating me like I had an infectious disease. They tried everything in their power to get rid of me. One afternoon, I decided to go out for the day with a girlfriend of mine. We went for lunch and then hung out by the pool at her condo. We had a really nice time together and despite my little paunchy belly I still looked pretty good in my bikini, which I was proud of. It must've been about 5 p.m. when I got home that day. I pulled up to the Noble House expecting to be greeted by the motley crew like always, but instead the whole place was empty.

A friend of the Bell family was standing in the middle of the empty living room with a letter in his hand. He handed it to me and just stood there with a smirk on his face. This was a goodbye letter written in Bob's handwriting, only they weren't his words. I couldn't believe what I was reading but I was sure that this is what Bob and his family must have thought was best for all of us. What? I started screaming and pulling the hair from my head. This was a complete nightmare, this was not happening, something wasn't right here. He would never leave me like that. The family friend left, and I immediately called Colleen at work. I barely got the story out to her and she was on her way to come and get me.

Colleen was still living in the house with Mum and Maureen. At this time Mum and I were still mostly on the outs. First I had lost my virginity and now, a couple of years after we had somewhat mended our relationship I was pregnant, but not married. I guess it was too much for her and just like before, she disowned me, whatever that means. Based on her overreaction to when I lost my virginity, this didn't surprise me. So what does Colleen do? She brings me to Mum's house, the same house I had lived in before meeting Bob. It was a three-story condo (that my money had contributed quite a bit to over the years). The first floor was the garage and that's where Colleen made me stay and wait while she went upstairs to break the news to Mum that I was there. She assured me that once she explained what had happened with Bob that Mum would come around. I expected to hear a lot of yelling, which at first I did. However, to my surprise, it didn't take long for Mum to take me back under her wing. She was going to have this baby "with" me. It would be her grandchild after all.

I must have been at her house for about a week when Bob's mother, also named Marian but spelled differently, called and announced to my mother that she had set up an appointment for me to have an abortion and after that was taken care of, it would probably be best if Bob and I never saw each other again. As I suspected, the abortion topic made it outright war. "How dare you put my daughter on the chopping block?" It was on! Marion Buck versus Marian Bell! Now my heart was still with Bob, and I just couldn't believe that these were his wishes at all. We had talked about our dreams of getting married on horseback at the beach with lots of flowers all around and all that good stuff. I had a deep need to speak with Bob, but no one at the Bell house would take my calls. However, I remained determined. I rang that house like crazy.

In the meantime, I decided to pay a visit to a clinic. Maybe it would help me figure out what to do. After I arrived at Planned Parenthood I was asked by the main counselor if her trainee could sit in on our interview. I was so confused at the time, it didn't matter to me who was in the room. In walked her trainee and I can only describe her as looking like Mary or at least the pictures I had seen growing up of Jesus' mother. Throughout the interview, I felt the counselor was focusing more on the abortion option. Then I would look at Victoria who kept giving me looks that said, "Come on, little sister. You know what's right for you." I went home that evening more confused than ever. Later that night, I received a call from Victoria. She told me that she had been fired that day from the clinic. Apparently, she had been caught stealing my file. She explained that she was a married woman with three children of her own. She promised me that if I kept this baby, she would do everything in her power to help me. Knowing that I had at least one person's support, I agreed and she kept her promise. She provided me with lunches, spiritual literature, and even played classical music to my stomach.

With my newfound confidence about the pregnancy, thanks to my angel, I was determined to get in touch with Bob and at least let him know about the baby. One afternoon, as luck would have it, one of Bob's brothers answered the phone. Somehow, he had no idea what was going on and he let the cat out of the bag. All along, the family had me believing that Bob had left the state. His brother informed me that Bob was actually living in an apartment off Sherman Way in the San Fernando Valley. I remembered that Bob and I had once looked at a place over there so I knew exactly where it was and where to look. Sure enough, I found it. As I suspected, all the things that he had said in the letter had been flat-out dictated to him by his parents. He had been forced to leave me. I couldn't tell Mum that I had found him, because that was part of my promise to her—that if she helped with the pregnancy I'd never see him again. I wanted Colleen to know, though, so I wrote her a note in our secret language and left it on her bed. Well, go figure. Mum found it and deciphered it and I was immediately kicked out of the house. Again.

That's another pattern that repeated itself throughout my childhood and young adult life. Family love and acceptance. It was always conditional and based on how I acted or the choices

Run, Holly, Run!

I made. I didn't have that unconditional bond that others talk about. If my choices were not in line with the expected, I was out. Of course this was at a time when I was no longer able to contribute financially, the way I had done while I was working, so the problem might link back to my money issues.

So Bob and I were now living together on Sherman Way. He worked at a hardware store and I stayed home being pregnant and planning our wedding on our now quite limited budget. Las Vegas was the cheapest way to go, so off we went. It was quick and low frills, not the special occasion that one might think. After all we'd been through and the family pressure from both sides, we just thought it was the best move for us and the baby on the way. We tied the knot on November 8, 1980. I was certainly happy that we were moving forward the way everyone expected, but I also couldn't help feeling an odd sense of regret. Maybe things were moving too fast.

Shortly after the ceremony, which was held at the Imperial Palace in Vegas, complete with gold plastic wedding bands that we pulled from the box that the minister's wife handed us, I began to experience false labor contractions that would land me in the hospital every three days or so. It was unexpected because I wasn't due for another few months. To make things more challenging, we were on a Medicare plan that covered admission to only a few specific hospitals. I remember one particular hospital that was like a dungeon. I think they had me in the basement or the boiler room. It was very dark and dreary.

To my surprise, my mother came to see me at this godforsaken place. I thought I was dreaming. The first thing she said to me still rings in my ears. "You're having a baby today." Her delivery was cold and matter of fact. I knew on the inside she was caring like crazy, but because of pride couldn't admit it to a liar like me. It wasn't just that I had chosen Bob over her, but that I had lied to her about it. I couldn't focus on all of that right then.

I was released from the hospital and went home to bide my time. The false labor started coming every night and finally, on November 20—less than two weeks after our wedding—I was able to go to a hospital that was really nice, the closest one to my house. Only this time it wasn't false labor. Our son arrived prematurely at only 6 months, a tiny 2 lbs. 8 oz. He was so small, but so beautiful. God had created a masterpiece. When I was young, I must have dreamed about him (just like the Aborigines do) because I already had his name in my mind: Christopher Michael. In spite of everything that had gone down, Mum was just beside herself with joy, and it felt good to see her so happy.

I so desperately wanted to get hold of my angel Victoria who had been so instrumental in my decision to keep this baby. I wanted to let her know that with her help, I had followed through with the pregnancy and despite some challenges, I had produced this incredible child. I soon discovered that the phone numbers I had been given no longer worked. I checked with Planned Parenthood and there was no record that a Victoria had ever been associated with them. I'm sure, though, that wherever angels go for their coffee breaks, Victoria sits back and watches in all her beauty, knowing that she helped in the delivery of a beautiful soul.

We knew we had a lot of struggles ahead of us. Chris stayed in ICU and because of the close proximity to the hospital I was able to bring in my breastmilk every two hours, as he, of course, didn't have the strength to nurse. I used a mechanical breast pump that we had rented. It was a lot of work, but I was determined to make sure our baby was as healthy as possible. After all I had been through with the pregnancy, I was not going to give up now. After two months and countless trips back and forth, we were finally able to bring our baby home.

By that time I was able to breastfeed naturally so I went looking for the pump that we had rented so that we could return it. When I found it, I realized that we would not be able to take it back. Bob had turned it into a bong if you can believe that. Oh, lord, help me. My breast pump!

Talk about full circle. Does it give you a flashback to *Pufnstuf*?

CHAPTER 10

Down on the Farm

*W*hen Chris was healthy enough to be moved and had a few months of stability under his belt, Bob's father, Alphonzo, announced to us that he had been shopping for a farm, had bought one, and that he wanted us to help run it. It turned out his own father had grown up on ranches. He had always dreamed of owning one but was tied up for the previous 17 years in Washington, representing the Marina Del Rey District. When I was offered the work on the Bell farm, I realized that my beautiful Mustang wasn't going to do me any good. Thank God my brother also handled the trucks at the Ford dealership, so I traded my Mustang in for a flatbed truck.

I wasn't acting anymore, just raising my son. So off we went. It was incredible. This 100-acre farm was located in Fallon, Nevada, which is about an hour east of Reno. The farm was divided into two operations. One was the dairy farm and the other the hog farm. This was no mom & pop shop, actually the complete opposite. The pig farm was all automated. Everything from the feeders to the flushing system, which fed, cleaned, and watered all the hogs. A crew of about eight people completed all the rest of the duties that the machines could not. For instance, the team performed physical check-ups, administered required medications, and managed the constant relocating of the hogs.

There were ten different barns and the hogs were moved to the appropriate barn at various stages of their lives. We produced

Run, Holly, Run!

12,000 hogs a year. My husband and I did work the hog farm for a period of time. We had to learn all aspects of the farm. I'll tell you what, though, you have never smelled anything as vile as the inside of one of those barns. The smell would stick to you like glue. Your car would smell like it and of course your clothes. We had a rule that all clothes were removed before entering the living quarters of our home.

When we moved to Fallon, my son Christopher was about six months old. In order for both Bob and me to work, we were going to need a nanny. So I called a service in town (I couldn't believe they actually had one). Into our lives stepped Fran Ham. What a character. Straight shooter, a tell-it-like-it-is kind of gal. Right away she and Christopher bonded and that was really all I cared about. At the time we were just renting a house in town. Besides taking care of Christopher, Fran's duties included light housekeeping. For that town and the scarcity of jobs, she was making really good money and we treated her very well, like one of the family.

We spent about six months at the hog operation, which was located at the back of the ranch by the mill. The mill was supplied with truckloads of different grains pretty much all day. The silos were never full for long. We went through tremendous amounts of food. Although we worked a number of different jobs, the dairy was where we spent the most time following the six months with the hog operation. My first job in the beginning of our time at the dairy was feeding the calves. The milk barns were also au-tomated, except for the cleanup which involved a hundred-step procedure that lasted two hours and was done twice a day between milk shifts. I now know my way around a farm, that's for sure. I've even delivered many a calf.

It was during this time, that I began seeing more and more of Bob's anger and I wasn't sure what to do. Things were getting progressively worse. I decided to try to focus on our relationship and sat Bob down for a talk. He told me he wanted to have five children. I wanted to make this work so I suggested a compromise. For now let's agree to at least one more. I removed my IUD and I remember making love the night after our talk. I purposely wouldn't let him touch me for a month after that because I wanted us both to know that I had actually felt the conception that night. It turned out I was right. A woman knows these things. The next eight months were unbearable, though. The problems started on my second visit to the doctor. It was then that I was informed that I had a sexually transmitted disease. I immediately started crying because I just knew that he had cheated on me. I didn't know when or where, but there had been some betrayal somewhere along the way. Bob denied it. Let me rephrase that. He lied. He tried to convince me I had picked it up from a Jacuzzi or a toilet seat or something. Only he had it, too. But this kind was no big deal for men. No big deal at all. But for a pregnant woman? It's one thing to have an STD when you're strong and healthy. It's a whole other beast when you're pregnant because they can't treat it in the same way.

During this time, I was brought into the farm office to work. Compared to what I had experienced working outside in 20-degrees-below weather, you'd think this would be a cake walk. Well, not for me. In the office I was greener than the alfalfa we fed the cows. But what I haven't mentioned yet is the fact that both of my sisters by that time also worked in the office. After the first year of being in Fallon, I began to get homesick. I was really missing my family, especially Colleen. So she was my first target to get out there. It wasn't easy. I had to convince her to leave L.A. and her job. "Come to Fallon" was not an easy sales pitch. Colleen took a leap of faith, moved to Fallon, and became the next employee at Bar-Bell Farms.

As much as I had grown to love the Bell family and my husband, I needed a piece of my world and Colleen was just what the doctor ordered. It took longer to convince Mum and Maureen to take the plunge, but eventually they came as well. They had a house to sell and were planning on building a new home in Fallon. Colleen had experience as an administrative assistant so she showed me the ropes around the office. As Al's receptionist I definitely needed some training.

Each time the phone rang, I heard, "Is Alphonzo there?"

"Nope," I said and hung up.

He called back. "Hello?"

"He's not here. Bye."

Colleen saw that I needed help. "You're supposed to answer, 'Bar-Bell Farms. Who's calling? Can I take a message?'"

It was great having my own family there because Al could be a pain in the ass. Not only was I now his assistant, but I was also his unofficial counselor. When he placed a bed in his office to help me with my morning sickness, I thought that was a great idea. Then I realized that it was so he could confide in me while I was a captive audience. There was no escape. Now, mind you, this was a millionaire, an intelligent congressman, and he wanted to talk to me, not an actual counselor. I was pregnant and sick. I just wanted to do my work and be left alone, but no dice. He told me once, "You know, if I'd met you when I was younger, you'd be my wife today." That may sound weird but it really wasn't. It was a very genuine sentiment.

That also circles back to another issue that has followed me throughout my life, and you probably know what that is. Men. I would guess that it all stems from not having a father around when I was a child. I didn't really even have a substitute father figure in my life, because my brothers were older and mostly doing their own thing. That is until *LOTL* and Spencer came along. He certainly filled that void for me that I didn't even realize was there. But then he disappeared quickly and I was left with a traumatizing replacement.

As I got older, losing my virginity and later getting pregnant didn't bring the joy that I thought a relationship with a man was supposed to bring. Those were to be special, meaningful moments in my life, but instead they only brought me a lot of drama with my family and later with my in-laws. Now once again I found myself with an older man in my life who had become close to me, sort of fatherly in a way. Despite what he'd said, I think he was trying to express how close he felt to me and how he trusted me, which felt good. It felt real.

One benefit of this new office job of mine was that anytime Al was traveling and my counseling services were not needed, Colleen and I had free rein. She and I would literally run out the door and breathe in his dust as he drove down the washboard road leading from the farm. We would then put the answering machine on and make a break for town. Usually we would go by the house that Bob and I lived in, grab Christopher and take him out with us for a couple of hours. There were, however, times when we just went into town, got our nails done, or even did a little "ching chinging." This was Nevada after all and slot machines are everywhere, even in the restrooms. The saying, "Home is where you hang your hat" is so true. As long as Colleen was around, I never felt homesick. Not only was Colleen a Bar-Bell employee, but so was half the town.

Eventually Al Bell hired a contractor and took the relatively small dairy farm that he first purchased and sunk another $6 million into it. This farm was state-of-the-art. Even though much of the town was on his payroll (I was responsible for writing their checks), it took a long time to gain the town people's respect. They thought he was just some rich guy throwing money around. What they didn't realize was that Al was a true cowboy. He spent a lot of time in Colorado at the first Bar-Bell Ranch. Al's brother-in-law was Elliot Roosevelt, and he and Al's sister had a ranch in Colorado where Al spent time on their dude ranch. In fact, Al was still riding horses well into his seventies.

On Al's farm was a beautiful yellow and white two-story house. The interior had been remodeled by Marian and she made this seven-bedroom home gorgeous. She sometimes took me furniture shopping with her. She and I picked out all the wallpapers for the house. At the time, she and Al owned homes in L.A. and another big citrus farm in Ojai, CA. Each of them had been decorated by Marian and were just exquisite.

Al spent most of his time in Fallon and Marian came up maybe every couple of months. This schedule that the Bells had would at times leave that great big beautiful house empty. That's when the big Bar-Bell parties would kick into gear. And Bob and I sure knew how to throw some rippers. We had credit accounts at a majority of the stores in town. Getting supplies to throw a hellacious party was no problem. The farm had all the toys, too. Bob saw to that. We sometimes even had live bands.

At this time in my life I never had to worry about money. Maybe that was a good thing, or maybe it only helped feed into my distorted view of money and power, but it was intoxicating. Not only did we have the accounts in town, Bob and I made a healthy combined salary. Another bonus was Bob's trust fund. We received a check every month on the interest of a quarter of a million dollars. That in itself was a large amount. We were very young to have that kind of money. Bob had always known that kind of wealth, but for me this was new. My rich/poor cycle was currently on an upswing.

I took care of the bills, the taxes, and for the most part the spending, except for Bob's toys. If he didn't get the money from me, he would get it from his father; in the end he got his toys—usually something with an engine. One time, Bob and I got into a huge fight. A few months before this blowout, Bob had purchased an all-terrain vehicle that was actually quite cute. It had roll bars, nets, and a racy paint job. It looked like a large toy. Bob wound up taking that cute toy apart, putting about two grand's worth of junk on it and ruining it.

One morning I arrived at the farm and saw the workers pulling out of the ranch in the truck that carried all the deceased animals to a pit. I stopped the truck and told the guys to load that piece of junk ATV into the back and take it with them. So off it went. That was a bold move for me and it started a huge fight between Bob and me. It wasn't only this fight, but plenty of others that seemed to escalate and become more frequent. I wasn't sure what was going on, but something wasn't right.

Later I went into town to go to the bank. I was driving the truck that was used to haul bottles of milk, which would inevitably splatter and draw flies. I pulled up to the drive-through window. The bank clerk opened the slot and I rolled down my window as about 20 flies shot out. She began flailing her arms at the flies that had found their way inside. It made me pause for a minute. Here I had gone from being like a celebrity in Los Angeles to basically driving a milk truck filled with flies. However, that wasn't my only moment of clarity. When I asked her how much money I had in my personal account, she said I had $1,000. Really? I didn't realize that checks don't always clear right away. Prior to the years with Bob, other people handled my money so I was on a huge learning curve. It takes time for a check to clear. Okay, now I know. Thinking I had $1,000, when the checks I had already written simply hadn't cleared the account yet, meant I spent that $1,000 a second time. I wound up costing myself probably another thousand making all of those checks good.

So not only was I learning how to manage money, but I was dealing with this health issue. Every month of the pregnancy, during the visit to my doctor's office, they'd burn the lesions or cysts or whatever off ... but they grew right back. Bob always went with me, but still I always cried because I knew he was lying to me. The last month they couldn't burn me anymore and no one could reassure me that everything was going to be okay. And it wasn't. In fact, I nearly died. During the birthing process my placenta shattered and my cervix went into spasms. I had to have blood transfusions. Luckily, through some miracle, my an-

gels saw Phonzo through the ordeal to arrive without any problems on his part.

As far as cheating, Bob had denied everything up to that point, so I was just supposed to believe that this rotten infection had happened to me randomly out of the blue. Down the road, he finally copped to the affair with the bank clerk. I know what you're thinking and you are exactly right. It was the same woman who was attacked by the milk flies at the bank drive-through. Maybe that had been a sign. I know I shouldn't have done it, but I eventually approached her. It was a very small town. She said, "Sorry you can't please your husband." You know what? He might have been with you for one night but he banged on my door to get back in the next day and I certainly wouldn't hold my breath on him banging on yours. How much more pleasing did I have to do?

So, shortly after the birth of our second son, my marriage was one camel stick away from breaking. I was in such inner turmoil at that time, recovering from the STD, the complications it had catapulted into the pregnancy, and the inevitable explosion that it had caused during the birthing process. I was so confused. I hated and loved my husband both at the same time. I hadn't yet come to realize that I was living with a man who didn't love— or even like—himself, much less me.

Looking back now, it was a classic case, really. I was so convinced that the problem had something to do with me not being pretty enough, not being sexy enough, or not being good enough in any and all aspects of my being. Why on earth do so many of us beat ourselves up with that God-awful, self-doubting hate stick?

I was searching desperately for some small sliver of self-confidence, so I decided to start a rock-n-roll band. I, of course, wanted to be the lead singer. Colleen was on keyboards, her husband was on drums and we stole a guitarist from another local band. Yellow Dog Fever was the name I selected for the group. The way I decided on it was by closing my eyes, opening the dictionary and pointing to the first word I could find. In its earliest stages, even Bob had shown an interest in joining the band, but that was quickly shot down because of his total lack of guitar skills. He didn't take the rejection well. One night, during one of our rehearsals, Bob came into the garage and announced that he was planning to throw a hellacious party out at the ranch house, the main house at Bar-Bell Farms.

Bob the "Party Coordinator" began by ripping out the custom stereo system from the walls of our gorgeous sunken living room. He then proceeded to cruise the streets of our small town, inviting anyone who was willing to consume mass quantities of alcohol and miscellaneous drugs. His last stop in town before heading out on the 10-mile trip to the ranch was at our bank, where he completely cleaned out our savings account. Now I'm not talking a few thousand dollars here. We had a lot of money in those days.

I don't recall what time it was the next day when he finally came slithering in, but needless to say, I greeted him with some choice words. Unfortunately, this was all he needed to refuel the fire. It began slowly with a couple of holes punched through the walls but escalated quickly from there. Our beautiful four-poster bed quickly became a no poster bed with the posts being used to smash and break everything in his path. I tried to stay out of the way of all the flying debris as best as I could, but then he brought out the rifle. That was the game changer. At that moment, I was so glad the boys were staying with their grandparents! He had already ripped all the phones from the walls. He began going from room to room, shooting out windows and blowing holes through family portraits. He made sure that one bullet found its way right through my heart in one photograph of me.

The weekend before this living nightmare, we had had a guest staying with us and I had set up a temporary phone for them in the guest bedroom. Thank God I remembered that because, without it, I have no doubt that I would have ended up in the same condition as my portrait. Instead, while his rampage continued, I managed to make one call out to Colleen without him noticing. Then I hid underneath the desk in our office and pulled the chair in to cover me. I watched as his feet walked right by me several times, but he was so into his own rage that he didn't even notice me there. I stayed quiet, trying not to antagonize him any more then he already was. I couldn't believe this is what my life had come to. Then, after what seemed like hours, I heard the sound of Colleen's truck pulling up and I quickly made a dash straight out the front door.

To my surprise, my mother was with Colleen. Bob came running out of the house after me. He took one look at Mum and froze in his steps. He somehow managed to regain some of his composure and instructed her very loudly to get her "old fucking ass" off his property. We all did just that.

Believe it or not, Bob was never arrested for his outburst. Apparently, it isn't illegal to destroy your own property. I went back to the house about a week later to find what I can only describe as the Pirates of the Caribbean ride at Disneyland. The house was essentially destroyed. Bits of glass and shiny jewelry were all over the place, especially in the master bedroom (like that old lady in the bed in the Pirates ride) where he had also unloaded a couple of fire extinguishers. All in all, the amount paid for the contractor who had built our home to come back out and fix it came to $18,000.

This crappy, nightmarish behavior of Bob's had by that point become a pattern. We'd work very hard to obtain the nice things we had only to lose them all over and over and over again to his violent outbursts and childish tantrums. What wasn't so childish was the physical abuse that I endured. I realized that I had married a real Dr. Jekyll and Mr. Hyde because he could go from zero to 100 in an instant and I paid the price. On more than one occasion, his fists slammed me into another galaxy. It was horrendous and I couldn't understand how I had allowed this to happen to me.

Mum told me stories about her husband cheating on her. Remember, by the time she had me she was already 41 years old. A few years later, when she came to pick me up from school people sometimes said, "Your grandma's here." I replied, "She's not my grandma, she's my mother." There was that big a spread in our ages. I wasn't around during the days when she was in her prime. I had always figured that wasn't going to happen to me. My husband would never cheat on me because I'm pretty. I keep myself in shape and I'm working on my life ... yet I was going through the exact thing I had promised myself would never happen.

In some ways, Al was in complete denial. He knew what his son was like, but Bob was his favorite and from what I understood about the past, he just always paid to "make it go away" when Bob caused trouble. But because I challenged him, Bob completely shot up our beautiful house. I'm talking 5000 square feet, with all the beautiful little prizes in it. I think his father didn't want to take back possession of his son. He knew he had scored when he had dumped him off on me. It was such an embarrassment in the community though that Al came up with this brilliant idea to move us to Duncan, Oklahoma and have Bob work on an oilrig for Haliburton. Al had friends there so he was able to slide his son right into a position. Oh, what fun for me! Fallon suddenly became the excuse for Bob's unacceptable behavior. Surely he wouldn't behave that way if he were shipped off to another town. Can you believe the lengths people go to when protecting someone like that? So rather than leave him, I went to Duncan with him.

The marriage didn't last long after the move.

CHAPTER 11

Oklahoma Crude

*T*he seven months we spent in Duncan were so boring that it doesn't even deserve a lot of ink to describe it. I will say that the one thing that Duncan had going for it was the best damn watermelon on the planet—juicy, lovely, crispy, Black Diamond Watermelon (Fallon, on the other hand, had had the best cantaloupe). I ate an entire watermelon every day! It became my nightly treat.

It was one night during one of those watermelon gorge fests that Bob and I watched the Farrah Fawcett movie, *The Burning Bed,* where she suffers abuse from her husband. For some mental meltdown reason of mine, I thought that maybe that movie would deter Bob from ever raising his hands to me. However, it was worse than that. Watching that movie brought back those painful words from my mother many years ago. "You're never gonna be Farrah Fawcett," she had told me. I said, "I know! That seat is taken." When I used to get weighed on a daily basis, I'd get grounded if I gained a pound because I had a period or something. Grounded again! It was a control thing. Mum said, "Farrah Fawcett weighs 102 lbs." I was like 112 then. Farrah was also 5' 2". I was 5' 8" by the time I was 15! And to get grounded because I had a period and gained a pound? The ironic thing was, and this was what I realized that day, when my mother died and my fiancé left and I got sick, I finally weighed exactly 102.

About a week or so after we had watched that movie, Bob

got the bright idea to reenact that one scene where the husband cut all of the belts out of the car and then beat the woman. Thank god my stomach was full of watermelon at the time because some of those kicks to the stomach could have turned out a lot worse. The strangest thing was that while he was hitting me, he was reciting the dialogue from the scene in the movie, word for word. It really freaked me out.

While he was beating me, I got my mother-in-law on the phone. I was in Oklahoma and she was in Los Angeles screaming, "Stay on the phone! I've got the cops coming!" Just like in the movie. Bob left for L.A. that night in his truck and took with him the keys to the useless car he'd left me. For me, "That was a wrap." It was the beginning of my plan of divorcing him. A cheat and a liar I know go hand-in-hand and his hand no longer appealed to me. I didn't want to hold it anymore. I thought all that was behind me.

You know, that lucky bastard got away with that one, too. Like I said, I had his mother on the phone from L.A. while it was all taking place. She was on the phone with the Duncan police and she could hear me screaming over the phone. Even with all that, when the cops showed up I swear I could hear banjos playing; they were straight out of the movie *Deliverance.* One of them commented to me, "You know, sometimes women bring this behavior onto themselves, you hear?"

I know that I'm not the first to use a river as a metaphor for life, however I am going to use it as a comparison to the abuse I've experienced. "Go with the flow." Oh, I love this idea. It's my nature. And just like a river I've taken a wild course or two. I feel like I've experienced all the aspects of a river. I'm the water moving along, free flowing and having the time of my life. Then I become the stick that gets caught and starts piling up leaves behind it. I keep getting hit by the water, but I can't seem to move, can't get back in the flow. I feel the nudges and suggestions that I should move, but I'm stuck. I just keep letting the water that was my friend brutally hit me. When I can no longer take the weight of the buildup, I let go.

That was it. We all reach our breaking point and I should have probably reached it long before, but I thought things would change. Or maybe I hoped they would. I had the two boys, ages two and four at the time, and we made arrangements to get back to L.A. on our own. When I arrived, I found the sharpest attorney in Beverly Hills. Bob was about to get the Razzie Award for his latest performance. My attorney was going to fight for me and get me so much, he insisted. He had to see Bob's books, first. But eventually—after Bob hid the books— my attorney switched sides since the other side could afford to pay him more.

The divorce became a reality, though, so good riddance to bad rubbish, as Mum would say. Now this divorce was actually a pretty big deal as I was walking away from a lot of money; but at that time, after all I had gone through, I honestly didn't care. I ended up with minimal child support, but I couldn't continue to live in such unnecessary pain. I was starting off my adult years, and like others who have unfortunately been in similar situations, I needed to be very strong in all my decision-making.

Ten years later, I was at a normal gynecologist checkup when I was informed that the STD virus had manifested into uterine cancer. I was so crazed. The female doctor who had to deliver that awful news (the cancer word) actually crawled up into my hospital bed, held me tight and cried with me. She had just been through this same scenario the year before. But still the fears and memories hit me square in the face. I had thought I was past it all, but apparently that area of my body was an issue that still needed to be dealt with. In tears, my first thoughts went to how much money this would cost to get treated because at that point, I sure didn't have much left. However, there was one bright spot. My ex-mother-in-law came to visit me and when I told her, she simply asked, "When can she go in?" More than 20 years later now, I'm happy to get the report out that I'm still cancer-free!

CHAPTER 12

My Boys

*N*ow that I was free of married life and no longer working on that farm, I could focus all of my energy on my boys. Even though they were my focus, I was tethered to the Bell family since my ex in-laws of course wanted to be in their grandchildren's lives. I also found myself still wrestling with the fact that since they had plenty of money, they were able to wield their influence over me through the boys. In fact, they were masters at the money game.

Since day one, Christopher and I have been one and the same. He's always been my sensitive child. He would cry at the drop of a hat. He's not only extremely handsome but carries an aura around him of self-worth. Some would even describe it as arrogance. On his flipside, he's very true to his Scorpio sign and constantly stings himself. As a little boy, and especially being my firstborn, he received an enormous amount of attention. I literally used to carry him around like a sack of potatoes. He was just so easy. I took him everywhere—concerts, camping, amusement parks—and, of course, if I wasn't taking him places with Bob, other family members and even friends jumped at the chance to have time with him. Both Mum and Marian had special bonds with him, too. Phonzo was Al's favorite, though. It may sound weird but in families it's just a fact of life that some people have favorites!

By the age of two, though, Chris had contracted the music

bug. He loved himself some rock n' roll. One Halloween when he was maybe 4 years old, we dressed him up like Billy Idol. Years later, I was at a nightclub in Hollywood called The Cathouse and who should I run into? You guessed it. Billy Idol. He was there with a bunch of his biker friends and they were all super nice to me. I was invited for a ride down the Hollywood Freeway with all of them. We wound up at a condo belonging to one of them, just hanging out. I remembered I had a photo of Chris in my wallet and I dug it out and showed it to Billy. He got a big kick out of it and Chris thought that was pretty cool when I told him about it later.

When Phonzo was attending Hollywood Beach Elementary School, the principal, who always had his black Corvette parked out in front of the school, had a crush on me. Because of that, he loved it whenever Phonzo got in trouble because then I would have to show up at the school. One of those times, I got a call, I showed up, and we were sitting at a table that was about three feet tall, all squeezed into the little kid chairs. Pre-school chairs. As an adult, it's almost impossible to sit in one. So there was the principal, three teachers, Phonzo and me. I was sitting there waiting to find out what Phonzo had done and in a whispering voice that was loud enough for Phonzo to easily hear, the principal said, "Well, you know he's a little slow." I looked at Phonzo and he looked back at me like, "I am in so much trouble." And I started laughing!

He pointed out, "Mama, you're making it worse."

"Oh, no I'm not. You watch me work, you little son of a gun." Oh, no. They weren't getting away with that. His face was in shock because he knew he was going to be in trouble. Only he wasn't in any trouble because Mama's to the rescue. I couldn't stop laughing and they were looking at me like I was out of my mind.

"Let me just ask you a simple question, you simpleton. You

mean he stopped to smell the roses?"

And they asked, "What? What?"

I said, "What? Are you slow?" Back at you! Then I flipped them the middle finger, said "Come on, Phonzo! We're going home," and we walked out of there. You thought that he couldn't hear you? Don't you dare do that to my son? You might as well have pulled a gun out and put it to his head because you simply terrified him. You made him feel like he was going to go home and get punished.

My boys and I all have a weird connection to the movie *The Princess Bride*. We must have seen that movie at least 100 times. We'd already rented it and returned it over and over for six months, and then still watched it again at my friend's house. There we were, all watching it once again, and thinking it was just hysterical, as usual. My girlfriend and I were multi-tasking, painting our nails while the movie was on. Out of the blue, Phonzo said, "Oh, hey! I want mine painted black." Sure, why the hell not?

The next day, I had a Child Protective Services notice under my door because my younger son was sent to the principal because the kids were all making fun of him for the black nail polish and he was not having any of that. The school authorities thought that I had slammed his fingers in the door of my car. Of course, because that was the story he had given them. Why they were so stupid to believe that and why they would call Child Protective Services on me I don't know. It was just so crazy. Kids! You are one and then you have one and you never know who's who. Half the time it's the kid who seems to behave like the adult running the show.

During this time, the Bells were never far away. They decided to hire an old family friend who was about 35 years old to drive my boys back and forth to their tennis lessons at the club in downtown L.A. that was family-owned. Weeks went by without any occurrence, so I assumed everything was going just fine. It freed me up in the afternoons to do my errands. Then one night around five o'clock, just when we were all settled down watching TV, the phone rang and on the other end of the line was a heavy breather. I didn't think much of it, hung up the phone and went back to the show I was watching with the boys. Phone rang again. Same breather. Five minutes later, again, and then again, and then again. It went on all through the night! I would take the phone off the hood for a while; as soon as I put it back, the calls would start up again. Meanwhile, I hit *69 on the number to no avail. At about 5 a.m., after a harrowing night, the calls stopped. I waited until about 7 a.m., hoping someone else wouldn't call in between. Then I tried *69 on the number again. This time it entered, but to my ungodly surprise it was the kids' driver on the other end! I was mortified! The question I fired out of my mouth was, "How could you DO this to us?"

"Oh, I'm sorry, I'm sorry!" was his reply. "Please don't tell anyone." Then he told me that he'd been arrested that night, beaten and then raped by one of the officers! It was very surreal. He kept saying, "Please don't say anything to anyone about this."

I promised him I wouldn't. I just said that because I was trying to dig out any information regarding my boys and if he had ever hurt them in any way. His reply to my questions was that when he was being raped, he liked it. After that statement, I was off that call and immediately on one to my in-laws. A huge fight with the Bells ensued. I thought I was going to jump out of my skin at the thought that they would place someone like that in charge of my kids. From my so-called outburst, they deemed me too emotionally unstable to even have my own kids; they kidnapped the boys for a few days until I could settle down.

That was an episode I'd like to forget but never will. I hated them so much for that, and no matter how much I came to love them over time, no matter how much they helped out my kids and me, a part of me always will. Looking back, someone's head had to roll for their misjudgment of character in who they called a family friend. Too bad it turned out to be mine.

My boys were later again briefly taken away from me and this time it was their own doing. I was living in Washington and I had spent a lot of money to have them stay with me. They blew a really good vacation because they were bored and had nothing to do so they called their grandmother and told her that I had left them out in the woods freezing which was, of course, a damn lie. I had given them money and put them on a bus to go tour the city while I worked. But they lied just to get attention and because they wanted to go home. We had really good food and I had great plans for them there but they missed their friends or something and they blew it. Not me. It was totally on them that time. And the cops came out. I still bring it up to them every once in a while.

As the years have gone by, I remain extremely close with both of my boys, although Chris and I sometimes argue like cats and dogs. He tells me he likes it because he, too, feels we're one and the same. I don't think there are enough words to describe how much my son Phonzo means to me. He has shown me unconditional love and protection. I've spent so much time with him through music, reading, and just times when we sat together trying to forgive, understand, and know that we played the best game the dealer dealt us. We had some tough times but we love each other.

My kids and I are as close these days as three peas in a pod. We're like the Three Musketeers. We kicked their father out of the bunch. We don't need a fourth musketeer. These days they call him "Bob" which I think is the biggest slap in the face for a father; for your children not to say "Hey, Dad!" but instead to call you by your first name. My kids call me Mama. "Hey, Mama" They are the real, true princes of Bel Air. I want them to meet Will Smith and hand him their grandfather's book, *The Bel Air Kid*. Al Bell, Jr. was the original Bel Air kid and my kids are the only grandchildren he had. Christopher Michael and Alphonzo Robert Bell. They both live in Nevada. Trying to get on their journey. It's hard when you come from a lot of money and then have to struggle for the first time. The trust fund their father received after his parents passed on was never shared with either of his boys.

I hope you'll indulge me just a bit here but there's something I feel I need to do while we're all here.

Dear Bob,

I know you will probably find this letter to come from way out in left field—especially here—but, as all people do, sometimes you just get to thinking.

I remember on many occasions back when we were first married that you would be pushed to your boiling point. After all the anger had settled down, you would eventually break down and tell me the same story you had told me many times before. It was your memory as a 10-year-old boy of how angry you were when your dad remarried and you had to give up your bedroom to your new stepbrother. That loss and betrayal was devastating to you.

This letter isn't meant to make you feel guilty. My hope is that you will have empathy for the two wonderful sons that I know deep down inside you care for very much. As your heart once ached, theirs ache, too.

They are great men now with beautiful souls. I hope someday you will find it in your heart to not give up on them. With all of your shenanigans, no one ever gave up on you. Al and Marian died having never given up on you.

The boys cannot help but love you. I know personally what it feels like to not have a father, because I never met mine. I can only imagine their heartache, knowing their father only lives a state away. Please give this some thought.

Take care,

Kathleen

118

Run, Holly, Run!

Once, a friend of mine had a visitor who was a palm reader from India. I, of course, was intrigued but also apprehensive to meet with this man. I was a single mother with two boys. I was just beginning my attempt at my spiritual journey. I can't remember the palm reader's name for the life of me, but I do remember that he grabbed my wrists immediately. He looked at the rings around my wrists. I had three solid bands on my left wrist. I had three bands on my right wrist, with the band in the middle broken. The palm reader said the broken band described my financial future. He explained there would be a time when I may be physically or spiritually poor. He then began to speak of two males in my life. I had not mentioned to him that I had children. He said that in a past life, my younger son was my father, and my older son was my brother.

This made perfect sense to me.

CHAPTER 13

The In-Laws

*M*arrying into the Bell family took me to a whole other world. As you can tell, I had some rough times with my in-laws right from the beginning but in the end, I actually kept them a hell of a lot longer than I kept their son.

With all of his faults, Alphonzo Bell, Jr. was pretty amazing. He came from wealth and put it to good use. He and I both understood the philosophy that you start at the bottom and you learn everything about it. That way you can relate to everybody. You can relate to the person who rakes the leaves or cleans the toilet. You learn to do it all. Which I did. I did it all. The ranch was a great learning experience.

Al's second wife, Bob's stepmother, was the former Marian McCargo, who had been a tennis champ and then a movie and television actress for many years. One of her biggest roles was in 1969's *The Undefeated* where she co-starred with box office champs John Wayne and Rock Hudson. In 1970, when she married Al, he already had three sons and she had four sons of her own, including actors Billy and Rick Moses. It was like a Brady Bunch thing with seven boys in the overall family. Billy Moses was later on *Falcon Crest*. He did some movie about a pizza joint with Julia Roberts, too. The oldest brother, Rick, was on *General Hospital* during its peak of popularity and he also recorded music. Marian and I had our issues for sure, but in the end, what a lovely woman she was. She and I could get into some really good giggle sessions.

They took me in. It's almost unheard of. They took care of me for 25 years whenever I wasn't financially, spiritually, emotionally, or otherwise able to take care of myself, and believe me there's been a lot of that going on in my life. They would pay Bob to go away and they would pay me to come to them. Marian would call me and say, "Oh, I've got a new book. You've got to get it!" or I would call her and tell her, "Oh, I've got just the best thing for you today!" She was a minister—among a million other things that she was. I didn't even know she was a minister until ages later, but I used to go to church with her. I had a wonderful relationship with her. And not only was she good to me, but anybody I knew who got to meet her was completely touched. I always say I didn't graduate from my actual school. I graduated from the college of Marian … and that's not an easy college to graduate from!

One time, we were hauling a horse that Al wanted to give to Marian, and the damn thing tried to escape. There was a little window on top of the trailer we had. It wasn't much bigger than an air vent. The horse was apparently claustrophobic and it tried to jump out that window. So we had a horse that was halfway out of his trailer! The horse did survive, but he was not quite right after that. Hell, if he had been right, he never would have tried that in the first place!

Years later, when the two of them, Al and Marian, lay dying, I can honestly say I've never seen two people go more beautifully than they did. I was standing there in a room full of boys. All seven in the family were there including the one I had been married to. Al wiggled his index finger in a "Come here" gesture and I looked behind me thinking—hoping—he's calling someone else, but no. Of course not. He was calling me.

He called me over to his bed and I asked, "What the hell do you want?" in a funny way, of course. That was our relationship.

"I just wanted to tell you ... how much I love you," he managed to get out. Then he pointed at Marian who was also dying and he said, "Do you know how much she loved you?"

"Are you trying to make me cry?" I asked him.

He said, "No ... yes, yes." This is the cutest part and I hope that someday in your world you get one of these. He said to me, "And what about that damn horse?" Bringing up a moment that has nothing at all to do with life or death. Just a funny moment to bring it all back into perspective. Dying, crying. I was in an emotional whirlpool and he said, "What about that damn horse?"

When I was in that room, there was a lot of hospital equipment all over the place. After we'd had our good giggle, he said, "Enough. I want to hold her." Even then, when Al wanted something, he got it. Everyone grabbed something and moved it out of the room, ventilator or oxygen tank, or whatever. There was no purpose for any of it anymore. Get it out of the way. So we moved the beds together and he put his arm over Marian while she passed. Damn, that was beautiful. That's what it's all about. We were all just standing around in shock. A really lovely story. I'm thrilled that they went more or less together and as quickly as they did. I'm so happy because I know they were lovebirds. For them to be together again as quickly as possible made me happy. That part of it was all good to me.

I was just so very lucky to maintain my relationship with Al and Marian Bell, even after I was no longer married to their son. I don't know too many people who after a divorce can remain in the family. They were something else, all right. As I mentioned, there's a book called *The Bel Air Kid*, Alphonzo Bell's autobiography. When he was writing it, it was decided that none of his sons' ex-wives would be allowed to have their names mentioned in it. My children—his grandchildren—are in there, but I'm not. I told him he'd better write about me! He said there was one instance where he did. But then I got the book and he never mentioned me at all. He tells the story of us going to buy Marian that

horse, but he leaves me out of it. It still makes me smile that, in the end, he brought that up one last time. "What about that damn horse?"

In his own private way, he did sneak me into his book.

PART IV
REALLY
LOST

/

CHAPTER 14

Bad Days between Monsters

So I was 24, separated from my first husband and eagerly awaiting my final decree of divorce. I had my two boys with me, and a nice home. I'd been out of the loop for a long time so I thought I'd go back to my beginnings in entertainment. I went back to class and was taking it pretty seriously for about the first year until a guy named Phil joined the group. I was basically single and he was extremely handsome. What a combination.

We started to date on the sneak, or at least we thought so, but everybody picked up on it as if it was the flu or chicken pox. Despite all of our attempts at deception, we had let the cat out of the bag. We dated for many months and then decided to move in together. He was mature, sophisticated, and most of all, very good with the boys. Coming from the relationship I had just left into this one was a welcome bliss. He always seemed to do the right thing. He was a car salesman out of the Bay area but also had a secret desire to be a movie star. He certainly had the looks for it, but like many other dreamers he still was a salesman. He didn't have the heart of an actor. We were about two years into our relationship when he proposed to me. He took me to the finest jeweler in Beverly Hills and had my mother's diamond ring reset into our engagement ring. Weeks later I found myself trying on bridal gowns and I scored the most beautiful dress. Life was so good for a change. Everything was in perfect order.

Headed into happiness, full speed ahead.

During the seven months of our engagement, Phil and I managed to squeeze in many exciting events. At the time, Phil was working on a self-produced play, which he starred in. It was his attempt at showcasing himself to Hollywood. It provided an action-packed summer, what with all the rehearsals and camaraderie involved with a theatrical production. I introduced my old pal Moosie Drier to Phil and he wound up being cast in the play opposite him.

To get away, we went on many camping excursions with the boys during that summer and had plenty of backyard barbecues. Ping-pong tournaments and Slip'N Slides were of high importance at these get-togethers. It was around that time, though, toward the end of that great summer, that Mum took ill. Phil was moving to San Francisco and, of course, he wanted the boys and me to go with him. Only I couldn't go anywhere right then because I needed to stay for Mum. So Phil left without us. The reason he was moving in the first place was that his father had tricked him. Phil's father had started to put pressure on him to come back and run his business for him. He had a huge Chevrolet dealership in the San Francisco area. His dad was dying and yet he failed to ever mention that little fact to him. He only said, "I'm gonna start cutting off your credit cards. I'm taking your vehicle back." It just got to be too much. I was paying all the rent where we lived. He had a house in the Hollywood Hills but he basically stayed at my place.

He went back to San Francisco for a weekend. He was supposed to scout out schools for my kids and all that sort of stuff while he was there. Several times he called me to ask me to pick him up at the airport, but I'd go and he wouldn't be there. Then he'd call and say he was sorry, that he'd be on the next plane. And still he never showed, time and time again. He even sent apologetic roses.

I finally said, "I wonder, are you really not even coming back?"

Run, Holly, Run!

He said, "Maybe that would be best." He never did come back. My wedding dress was under my bed and my ring was on my finger ... and then my mother died.

I was 24 years old when Mum got sick. I had an incredibly hard time dealing with it. Mum had been not only my mother, but also my manager. Over time, our relationship was very strange. To the outside world, it may have appeared that I was spoiled. To me it felt like I was smothered. I just wanted to do things that all the other kids did, but that was not in the plan for me. I was segregated from normality. I knew Mum loved me very deeply. At times, I saw her talking to other parents about me and her eyes twinkled so brightly as if she had something so much more special than they did.

When we received the phone call that Mum was back in the hospital, Colleen and I immediately booked flights from California to Nevada. At the airport, we waited for our flight in a bar area. In my emotional stupor, I spotted some teddy bears on top of the shelf of the bar and I asked to see one. I bought it from them. Colleen thought it was sloppy and stupid on my part, but the female bartender came to my defense. When we finally got to the hospital, I proudly presented it to her. Over the next few weeks, we either drove up or flew, whichever worked best. During one of those visits, Maureen was already there and suggested that we leave the hospital so Mum could rest.

The next morning the phone rang and there was a nun on the other end declaring that Mum had taken a turn for the worse. She told us that we should make every attempt to get back to the hospital as soon as possible. The phrase "turn for the worse" has always meant to me that there's still time. Maybe short but nonetheless still time. The hospital was about three miles into town and when we went running out of the house, we were expecting to see our car. Only we'd both forgotten that this week we'd flown in and not driven like the week prior. So off we ran like a couple of gazelles being chased by a pack of lions. We were about four blocks from the hospital, exhausted, when a car pulled up in front of us at a crosswalk. In one of God's coincidences, it was our mother's doctor. He told us to get into his car and casually informed us that our mother was already dead. That hit Colleen and me like a tidal wave.

When we finally reached the hospital, I raced into Mum's room. There she was, lying with my teddy bear clutched in her arms. Even though some of her lessons were harsh toward me, Mum had always been my protector and now she was gone. Maureen arrived and took the teddy bear from her hands and gave it to me. I took it home and while my boys were little, they used to sleep with it. It made them feel included.

Everything was so super-duper devastatingly unbelievably crazy. Oh, my god. From that moment, I was paralyzed with pain and confusion. Of course, plans had to be made and all the emotions had to go on the back burner temporarily. Phil stayed with the boys during the week of funeral plans. I was hanging on by a string. Mum was put to rest. I came home to Phil and my boys for much-needed comfort and compassion and whatever else they could give me. I was so twisted in a knot. You're not going to believe this. When I was home for 24 hours, that's when Phil decided to hit me with it.

"I'm leaving you. I don't want to get married."

CHAPTER 15

And Your Little Dog, Too!

I had a sweet relationship with Tony. He was a guy who I met one night at The Rainbow Bar & Grill on Sunset Boulevard in Los Angeles. This club was a hot spot for rock n' rollers at the time and I believe it still is. Well, Tony came into my life while I was going through my long-hair-'80s-type-guy phase. He wasn't in a band although he was a musician. And since I was a gymnast, I really had an appreciation for his ability to dance. This gift of his was shared with my boys and we all credit him for their love of the art of dance (I do a pretty good jig, too, if I say so myself).

Anyway, Tony brought quite a bit of joy into our household just when we needed it. It didn't really matter that he was gay. In fact, that was never an issue, not with my boys and certainly not with me. We actually shared a very healthy sex life. We truly loved each other. I guess technically he was bisexual, but it felt to me like he had put his gay lifestyle on hold for the five years we spent together. They say that love breaks all barriers and that is exactly what happened with us. Tony and I were brother and sister, mother and father, lovers and best friends. We also shopped like giddy teenagers with newly acquired credit cards. He was great with hair and makeup and could cook, too, and not just in the sack. Also, Tony's mother and I got along wonderfully. One Christmas, she wanted to buy me a $500 purse. It was a cute purse but I had another idea.

"No, I want this Pekingese I saw recently. Same price." She told me I wasn't in a position to take on any more responsibility. "You've got the boys," she said. "Just raise the boys."

I told her not to tell me what responsibilities I could or couldn't handle. I wanted Peke-A-Boo! He looked like a Mogwai from the movie *Gremlins*. I swear he just looked so unusual. He was the perfect Pekingese but he was so odd-looking, especially to people who weren't familiar with the breed. Maybe it was because of the movie, but to them he looked like Gizmo.

"I will pay you back next week when I get my paycheck but could you get him, please, because he's gonna be sold and then I'd just die." So I rode Tony's ass all day long until he insisted to his mother that she just had to get the dog. So she did. In the long run, she even ended up referring to herself as the dog's grandma.

While my relationship with my new dog was amazing, Tony and I realized that while we were having a great time, it wasn't meant to be forever. I'm sure our youth played a big part in dreaming it could last and I'm grateful for the experience. Without any police involvement, bruises, or any of that other stuff that came with the closure of my other relationships, this one ended civilly. We are still good friends and to this day Tony still says, "I know I live a gay lifestyle but you are the love of my life." How weird was it that gender never played a part in our relationship? He was just a really good person. Who gives a darn if you like one gender more than the other? As long as people are laughing and happy that's what it's all about. However, I did find a new friend in Peke-A-Boo.

One time an artist friend of mine had a showing in Los Angeles at a museum on Melrose. For years, I had asked him to do a painting of Peke-A-Boo. He told me he couldn't because Peke-A-Boo was "anatomically incorrect." He finally did relent and lo and behold, my little angel was the focal point in a 10 by 14 painting at his exhibit. "Grandma" and I took Peke-A-Boo to see it. He was the guest of honor!

Peke-A-Boo Jones remains the great love of my life. He taught me more than anybody that I'd ever come across before or have since. When I came to the door, he never said, "Hold on and let me put my groceries down." His first obligation was to love me. Is that not the most beautiful thing in the entire world? He never said, "Well, hold on a minute. I'm on the phone. I'll get to you in a minute." He taught me lessons in what it's like to really be true to yourself, how to treat people right, and how to be a good person.

I had the luxury of having him for 12 years.

"Peke-A-Boo Jones," my absolute Angel

CHAPTER 16

On the Beach

*W*e had been living in Beverly Hills for about two years when I freaked my kids out one day and made the announcement we were moving. I packed up everything and headed to the beach and that's where our whole other life started. We moved into a cute little beach house. I enrolled the boys in school and they immediately started making friends with the local surfer kids. At first, Chris had a very hard go of it because he was a very handsome, charismatic young man. Some of the other boys thought their girls had eyes for him. As you can imagine, that didn't go over well. Eventually though, the boys' common interests won out and both my kids joined the ranks of the surfers and skateboarders on Hollywood Beach.

It was a true community there. Bulk was a guy who looked exactly like Hulk Hogan. Hulk = Bulk. It's so lovely to think of him. For a few summers, he was camp counselor to my boys and took them on many excursions. He called my dog a Nazi gargoyle after Peke-A-Boo bit him. Bulk had a wicked sense of humor and was very entertaining. My thoughts just went to him. If I mention "the beach," Bulk's name just has to come up. He passed on not long ago but came by and spent some time with me beforehand. He knew he was dying and I think he just wanted to take some warm memories and laughter with him.

I certainly ran that beach while I lived there. That was a good time. It's one of the coolest beaches. It's in Oxnard, California, and it's called Hollywood Beach. Back in the '40s and '50s, the celebrities all had homes there. Right across from me was where Bogart lived. All the little houses had signs hanging out front hinting at who had once owned them, mostly old Hollywood actors. Hence the name, Hollywood Beach. In front of Bogart's house the sign read "Casablanca." Now what they're doing is taking down the little cottages and putting up these monster houses. First of all, it's rude. They're blocking the view. What do you need these big honking houses for if there are only two of you? They've just ruined it.

Those days on the beach were so lovely, though. I was in my late 20s to early 30s and I went an entire year without using money. The barter system. I'd do what I could do for one person and they'd do something for me. You babysit my son and I'll babysit your kids this weekend. I'm exaggerating by saying I never spent any money, although the majority of what we did then really was through bartering. It was one of the rare times when I felt free from the chaos that sometimes comes with money. This time things were much … easier.

In the marina there was an Australian store, although the likelihood of that was kind of weird to me. But the woman who ran the store had my mother's eyes and she took to me. The minute I walked in, I saw a painting on the wall that I had to have, *The Night Watchmen*. I told her I wanted that painting but it was $700 and I couldn't afford that. She told me I could go ahead and make payments. So I got a job working at the local burrito shop. I worked for seven months to pay for that picture. I was making $7.00 an hour and I only worked for 3 hours a day on the lunch shift. I wanted that painting so badly (it must be that Aussie blood of mine) and then I finally got it. I had it for a little while and then I turned right around and gave it to a total stranger! I believe in the "move it around" process.

That's when I started to really explore my love of art and painting, something I'd always felt but had no time to pursue. A lot of my artwork was influenced by a book called *Mutant Message Down Under*. Not only did the book take me in that direction but it also taught me so much about art and spirituality, which I incorporated into my own works.

The story of the first painting I sold, *The Birthing Tree,* goes like this. There was a guy who had a little mini-mart in Australia and there was a tree that used to be where his mini-mart was. They took down the tree and put up the store. The aborigines kept coming in there so he took the least popular stuff and put it on the aisle, where they would sit and dream of their children. It was a dream tree. The storeowner said, "They're coming in there dreaming of their children. Well, that means more customers for me. Bring 'em on!" So now I drew a dream tree with all the babies in it and a woman came into my beach house and saw it.

She said, "I am not leaving without that painting."

I said, "No that one's not for sale. I'm not selling that one." It was above my fireplace.

"I'm telling you I'm not leaving without it."

"You're only going to hurt my feelings with what you're going to offer me so I can't sell it."

She responded, "I'll give you $750 for it."

I immediately shouted, "Sold!"

So here I was paying $700 and working for seven months to buy a painting and then when I finished mine, *The Birthing Tree*, it sold for $750! I made $50 that I could use to buy supplies.

One day, I told one of my friends at the beach, "You know what? It's the strangest thing. I think I'm like one of those artists living on a beach."

"You idiot!" she replied. "You *are* one of those artists living on a beach!"

My house there was the party house. Everybody came to my beach house. That was a great thing. We had Fred Flintstone furniture and futons and a big fire pit out front. It was a wonderful, lovely time. Lots of music. Right across the street from where I lived was a restaurant called the Whale's Tail where I had once worked. One night I went over and sat down next to a guy at the bar who looked for all the world like Sidney Poitier. He started telling me that he had had the best day that anybody could ever wish for. I said, "You think so? I'm gonna make your day better! I want you to come home with me. I have something to give you." I scared the shit out of him. "No, you have to come home with me in order to get what I want to give you!" Everything I said made him think worse and worse of me. He had to have thought I was going to attack him or something. It all sounded so sexual but really it was not. Eventually, he came over and I pointed to the painting and said, "That's for you."

He said, "I can't take that."

I replied, "You have to. Allow me to be the icing on your wonderful day."

And he agreed.

CHAPTER 17

Second Time Around

I was working at the burrito stand when I met a guy who used to come in every day and order the same fish tacos or whatever the hell it was he ordered and he kept asking me to go out with him. I wasn't in dating mode. I was about 30 or so by that point. I finally said okay but it was really awkward and uncomfortable. We went to a reggae concert. Pretty harmless. Steel Pulse. Turned out to be one of my favorite bands later on.

He took me on so many exciting adventures, which was very cool. The two of us really went everywhere. You know how some people go to work all year and then they have a week's vacation? Sometimes we went to more places in just one week than most people go in an entire year! And that was an ongoing thing. We did that every single week! Fishing or camping or traveling or sailing. Amazing things!

Where were my kids during this time? Well, Bob had moved out to Phoenix, Arizona and for one semester of school and a summer they stayed with him. They were about 12-14 and starting to get a little on the frisky side. By that point, the boys were pretty close to me in height and weight. At times it was difficult to discipline them. They could look me straight in the eye. I thought they could use some Dad Time.

The guy I had met had a sailboat and so did I. We'd take our sailboats out together. One time we even saw a pod of about 75 blue whales! They're the largest animals that have ever lived on the planet and they're still alive. They're never ever in this area but for some freaky, freaky reason they were and they had their calves with them. The T-Rex could walk through the jawbone of these things! Their tongue is the size of an African elephant. To see them in reality, we were just crying. I've been around dolphins out in the ocean as far as the eye can see, while the dolphins were leaping out of the water like they were celebrating. It was all so surreal.

We had a deep spiritual connection and the same wanderlust mentality. We had really made a connection and it wasn't long before he was husband number two. We were married at a place called Jalama Beach northeast of Santa Barbara. It was a decidedly intimate affair, just him, me, my friend Bulk, the minister, and of course Peke-A-Boo Jones.

One thing I couldn't figure out was where this guy's money came from. I had been working and saving, but he never seemed to work. He came across as just incredibly mellow. "They call me mellow yellow. That's right." Like my first husband, walking around the house, so calm. He would talk about communes, he was all into this metaphysical stuff, we read books together, went camping all the time. Maybe he had inherited his money, I wasn't sure, but we were having a good time so I was trying to "go with the flow."

Turned out he smuggled drugs before I met him. Yep, he was a drug smuggler. He used to stuff balloons filled with cocaine up his booty! He was able to buy himself the sailboat with the proceeds. I was not aware of any of this in the beginning, and when I did find out I was already in yet another bad situation. Let me explain.

I was with this man for six years and at first the travel and free lifestyle was exciting and alluring. We seemed to get along so well and things came easy for us ... at first. Then I started seeing the same old signs, but much worse. Once again a man was determined to control me and my actions. So now I was getting treated horribly all over the place: Nevada, Utah, Washington, Arizona, even down in Mexico. It was a hellacious prison that I could not escape.

One day we were driving around like usual and pulled over at a beautiful lake, nobody around; we had the place all to ourselves so we were fishing in the nude. Free spirits. We were basically homeless at that time since we just didn't have a house. We were always traveling. The lake served not only as a fishing hole, but also as a bath and a place to unwind before we had to hit the road again. That's just how we did it when we could. We would drink for a while, sleep to sober up, and then get behind the wheel again. At one point, though, he decided that I'd had enough to drink so he locked the ice chest up in one of the trucks. At that time I really loved my beers and it would irk me to no end when he'd start doling them out to me one by one. I guess it was the control issue. I was still being told what I could and couldn't do.

We were traveling with two pickups. The truck I was driving had the ice chest in it. I remembered that we had tied a spare key underneath the truck so I crawled underneath to snatch the hidden key. Well, when he saw me, he jumped into the truck and literally ran me over! He knew I was under there and was trying to get out of there! Thankfully I was able to avoid the wheels as they roared by me. He then got out of the truck, locked it, jumped into his other truck and took off, leaving me there completely naked. No clothes, no keys to the truck. Just totally and completely stuck.

After a few hours went by, it became obvious that once again he wasn't coming back for me (yes, it had happened before). I figured I'd better hike up to the road to get some help. Mind you, I was trying to cover myself up and simultaneously flag someone over to help me, not even knowing what kind of creep mass murderer would stop … if anyone! Thank God that after about an hour a car slowed down. It was a woman driving and all she said when she saw me was, "Domestic violence?" I nodded yes. Finally I heard her say something that sounded like she was going for help. I climbed back down to the truck and just waited. It was pretty far out from the nearest city. After what seemed like an eternity, I finally heard a vehicle pull up. It had gotten dark by then so I could hardly even see what it was but it was an ambulance or some sort of an emergency truck.

Two young, good-looking, male Sheriff's officers stepped out and headed straight toward my naked ass. I was trying to use the truck to cover myself up. They were so nice to me, though. After the initial embarrassment of my nakedness, one of the guys gave me a coat to wear, covering me up and calming me down before asking me for my autograph. I'm never sure how the subject of *Land of the Lost* gets brought up. Yeah, sure. It's probably my doing. I'm just lucky that these saviors were fans. I had nothing else, not even a stitch of clothing, but I still had my past, thank god!

Did I mention that inside the camper (still attached to the truck) was not only my best friend Peke-A-Boo Jones but also our lop-eared bunny, Wailer, as well as our cat, Ramona? The guys called for a tow right away, but having this combination vehicle proposed a huge headache. It couldn't be towed by a normal tow truck. Oh, no. That would have been too easy. It needed a flatbed specialty truck. So it was another few hours of waiting with them for the tow. It was during this waiting period that the whole autograph scenario occurred. I found an 8 x 10 picture of me as Holly and signed it for one of the guys. He was thrilled. What else were we going to talk about?

Eventually, the vehicle got picked up and delivered to a Denny's parking lot and on their merry way went the officers. I knew that's where I had to go because we had been there before and I knew my husband would return there. They had been able to get the truck unlocked with keys from inside the camper. Two days later, the bastard finally showed up just as I had expected. It seems he had taken off to Vegas after he left me and wound up getting arrested due to his fabulous ethics and personality.

Another time, I was left in the desert somewhere between Utah and Nevada. It had been so cold outside that, even with the truck heater on, I was luckily still wearing my parka. When he kicked me out of the truck that time, I was at least dressed warmly. I had my cigarettes and, more important, my lighter. I also had some weed in my pocket. I knew he was going to come back and get me. He couldn't just leave me there. But he didn't come. After many hours of waiting, the night and the cold air it brought set in. People assume that the desert is always hot, but when evening comes it's really just the opposite. I thought, "You're not gonna kill me!" So I built a rock ring fire. I gathered some twigs and branches and started the small fire with my trusty lighter (it was like a bad *LOTL* flashback!). I don't know how many more hours went by, but somehow I was able to keep that fire going. Then I heard a vehicle pull up nearby and I thought, "Son of a bitch!" I assumed it was my husband but it wasn't. It was a sheriff.

"Ma'am?"

"Go to hell," I shouted, thinking that it was my husband.

"Now, Ma'am, I need to approach you." Apparently some trucker drove by and had called the local sheriff. In a very stern voice, he said, "Ma'am, are you carrying any firearms?"

I yelled, "This is my fire here, what are you talking about?"

"I need to search you."

All of a sudden I woke up to the fact that I had that weed on me. Oh my God, here we go again. He frisked me down and put me in his vehicle. On the way to the police station, I thanked my lucky stars that he didn't find it in the inside pocket of my coat. I'd never been mixed up with the law at that point, but apparently they actually help you if you're in a situation like I was. The sheriff liked me. He took me into town and there was a program they had that provided for a hotel for the night, and they give you a continental breakfast, and then sent you on your merry way. Well, the hotel owner, when I went in for breakfast the next morning, kept yelling that I was an environmentalist because I was on the freebie for the continental breakfast. His daughter was a humble young woman of 17 or 18 and she was standing behind him while he kept screaming. So I went back to my room and the daughter called me and said, "He doesn't mean to be that rude."

Then the sheriff called me to say he had arranged for me to travel with a family that was going to Vegas at three o'clock. Okay, my sister lived in Vegas. That worked. I had a few hours to burn before my ride was going to arrive. I had no money and no identification card. I made a collect call to a friend of mine in L.A. and asked her to wire some money to the one bank in this small community. The Bank Manager told my friend that without ID they could not provide me with the funds. My friend explained to the Bank Manager what had happened to me. The Manager agreed to process the transfer. They did, however, at least need a description of what I looked like. My friend said she wasn't sure what color my hair was at the time, but it probably had tumble-weeds in it, since I had spent the night in the desert. She also told them that I had great teeth. So I walked into the bank smiling and they said, "It's you!" So after showing my fangs at the bank, I had some money back in my pocket.

I was told by the sheriff to be on time for my ride to Vegas or they would leave without me, so I hurried back to the motel and stood outside waiting for the only ride to Vegas. I got in the car with the two chubbiest women you could ever find and there in the backseat, where I sat, was a beautiful 4-year-old blonde girl with the glow of an angel. I felt very awkward when I first got into their car, as you can imagine. Ten minutes into the drive, I heard some moaning noises coming out of the back section of the SUV. I looked behind me and saw a jumbo-sized 12-year-old boy curled up in a ball. "Excuse me," I said to the woman driving, "I don't think he feels very well." I suggested that maybe we should pull over and get him some fresh air. She barked at me that he was just fine. "No, he's moaning," I said. She shouted at him to quiet down.

We continued to drive and the moaning got progressively worse. All of a sudden, I felt something hot on my head and back. It felt like someone had thrown a bucket of beef stew on me. Poor ol' Jumbo in the back had thrown up all over me. My stomach is so sensitive and this stretched me to my tolerance limits. The horrible odor permeated the car quickly. I begged the women up front to pull over. Begrudgingly, they finally did. One woman wiped the boy down with the blanket he had been wrapped in and then threw it down on the side of the road. Barking orders again, she told him to get back in the car. She told him she didn't want to hear another word out of him. All the while I'm thinking, "Hey lady, I have beef chunks in my hair ... can I get some help here?" No compassion was shown to me. The SUV was leaving. I jumped back in. Over the next few hours, I began to mentally evaporate. I had this beautiful little girl with crystal white-blue eyes staring at me. Her beauty didn't fit in with this group, she must have been adopted. The music from the radio blended in with the periodic new moans from Jumbo.

They finally dropped me in Las Vegas. I never ended up seeing my sister. With the help of the Bell Family, I got a prepaid airline ticket to Burbank, California. I was put on a plane, beef stew and all. Everybody was looking at me like I was just the grossest thing ever. The flight itself was pretty much a blur. I was greeted in Burbank by my money-transfer friend who reluctantly hugged me and said, "Oh my God, do you ever need a drink!" I agreed. "Quick, quick!" So she took me straight to the nearest bar and I filled her in on all that I had been through in the past couple of days. All the while, a businessman in a suit, with a briefcase, kept staring at me from a few bar stools down. I threw him some dirty looks back. I told my friend, "If that guy says one word—one word! I am going off!" Oh no, he was coming towards me! I was so ready to fly off the handle when he put a $20 bill in front of me and said, "You know what? I have never heard a more intoxicating story in my life. The drinks are on me tonight." Crazy! But that is my life. Here I was, ready to punch him and he turned out to be just a nosy gentleman.

You would think I had learned my lesson, but I went back and we found ourselves in Mexico. We had gone out for the day in search of all the most beautiful spots we could find. We were equipped with our ice chest stuffed to the brim with "bianas," oversized beers. Everything seemed to be going fine. We had lots of laughs, lots of wows, and great food (he was a good cook). Around 8 p.m., though, "Raging Bull" reared his ugly head. Everything I said seemed to annoy him. His building rage led to bizarre, unexplainable actions. Around 10 p.m. that evening, he suddenly yanked me out of the truck and proceeded to duct tape my head. He bound my hands to my neck with the duct tape as well. The last thing I heard him say was, "Fuck you! Die, bitch!" Then I heard the sound of the truck pulling away.

I have no idea how long I was standing out there in the desert. I'm sure it had to have been for hours. Death for me seemed like a ticket that had already been purchased. I was just standing there waiting for a receipt. This was when God started working his magical tricks again. I thought I heard a vehicle drive up. Even after everything, I figured it had to be my husband coming back to save me. Instead, it was a stranger, a man with a Spanish accent, trying desperately to speak some form of English to me. I couldn't see a thing. My eyes were still taped shut. All I heard was "What are you doing out here?" and "*Vamonos!*" He was telling me to get into his truck in Spanish. "*Vamonos,*" was repeated over and over again as he began to peel the duct tape off my head. God, that pain felt so good. When I could see him,

I saw that he was about 55 years old.

In the distance, I could sort of make out a pick-up truck with some men in the back. The Spanish-speaking man started to pull me towards the truck. I kept pushing him away. My vision was blurry and I could hardly see anybody. All I could see of the truck was the silhouette of four guys in the back and two in the front and they were yelling at me. "Get into the truck!" And I was protesting, "No!" I knew what was going to happen if I got into that damn truck. In my twisted mind, I was still waiting for my husband to come back for me. How could I go with all of these men? My mind was racing with all kinds of fears of rape and eventual murder. I would never be found again. With every "*Vamonos*," the Spanish man would say to me that his wife was a good Christian woman. He must have said it 50 times. After about a half hour of this, I saw one man who wasn't Mexican stand up in the back of the truck and yell, "Oh, for crying out loud, get in!" For some crazy reason, that made me laugh. Because I started laughing and laughter is the cure for everything, I finally did get in with them. The man who spoke English told me that the guy who owned the truck had picked up all these men to give them a ride to their destinations. They were all hitch-hikers, basically, and he dropped them off at all the places that they needed to go along the way. What a nice guy. However, I was still terrified.

After the driver dropped the last man, he told me to hop into the front of the truck. Oh my God, now what? We eventually pulled up to what would be described as a lower-middle class house. He signaled for me to follow him. The door opened and I could see a large kitchen inside. There were children, young adults, and a woman at the stove stirring a pot. No one there knew what to make of me. They didn't understand why he had brought me there. The man signaled to the person I think was his wife, the woman at the stove, cooking beans or God knows what, to retrieve "*dos bianas* and *dos cigaros*" from the liquor

store down the street. When the woman turned from the stove, no kidding, she was wearing a shirt that said "Coca-Cola" and underneath that, "I Love Jesus." (A good Christian woman!) He motioned to me to sit at the picnic table they had in their kitchen. An hour went by, and my problems were being masked by the *bianas* that I was drinking so feverishly.

I was still convinced they were going to kill me. All of a sudden, the woman goes outside and carries back in a large box. Were they going to cut me up and stick me in this box? She began to raise her voice to me in Spanish and motioned for me to lie down on the kitchen floor. I knew it! I was scared out of my mind. I was in a foreign place and I didn't have any money. I dropped to the floor in the fetal position fearing my fate. I was so terrified. My hair was partially ripped out of my head, I was all dirty and she just kept yelling at me! Once again, God to the rescue in the most unpredictable manner ever. The woman dumped the contents of the box on me—a litter of adorable puppies! Because she knew I was just so afraid but puppies would make me feel better. I was in shock. With everything running through my head, I was a nervous wreck! What a beautiful idea! All the puppies were licking me and I could smell all that puppy breath and it just made me feel somewhat safe. And for her to think to do that … wow. I didn't know where the hell I was or who these people were who had found me in the desert. I was completely ass backwards in my thinking and for her to know exactly what I needed to calm me was just so lovely. So lovely. God bless her!

The next morning, they stayed true to their promise. When I had first gotten into his truck, he had said, "I'll get you back to where you need to go." It was nearly a two-hour ride but he promised he'd take me. At one point, he said, "I'll be back *uno momento*," and he went down the street. I found out later he had to borrow the money from a neighbor in order to pay for the gas! "*No problemo, no problemo.*" When we were ready to go, I went back inside and I hugged everybody goodbye. Even though I had been so scared at first, they had all been so nice to me. They wanted to see me off. The next thing I knew, though, they were all in the truck. They were all gonna go, too! How sweet is that? Here I was thinking I was saying goodbye to them and they were shaking their heads and smiling. Then the next thing I knew, everybody was right there with me in the truck!

When we finally got back to my home—I say home but really it was our campsite— I gave them all presents and we had a watermelon party (what is it with me and watermelon?). My rescuer whipped out some cocaine for himself. That was weird. I gave the little boy that came with us a Monopoly game and I gave the twin 17-year-old girls my two best dresses.

My husband was nowhere to be found, but all of our camping gear was there, and of course, our camper with the animals locked inside. After about an hour, I spotted you-know-who walking up a path from the beach carrying my surfboard. The asshole had been out surfing. It just boggles my mind every time I think of that. He really didn't care if I was dead or alive. The shock waves that must have gone through him when he saw me there smiling with my family of friends. Eat that!

I'll tell you the craziest thing. We ended up living in Mexico for three years and I left him many a time. But one phone call he made to me while we were separated was so strange because he said, "You know that village we went into?" I knew exactly what he was talking about. When we had visited this particular little village, the people there were put off by him. They were all handcrafters. I'm talking about old school handcrafting, not people just knitting or whatever. And he said, "After you left, I went back there again and I pretended to be like you. I pretended to have your energy." That was kind of a weird thing. He went into the village and he took on my persona and the people, he said, were so nice to him. But it wasn't him! He was pretending to

have my energy and he said, "I was never treated so nicely." Wherever I go, when I walk into a room or whatever, I treat people decently. It just comes back at me. But he pretended to be like me and he said," You can't believe how nice people were to me." But obviously he didn't learn a damn thing from that.

The asshole beat me and hit me in the face with a fire extinguisher. I still have the scar across my nose. He went to jail for that one and had a year's worth of domestic violence therapy. I was still living with him when he was going to those classes and after he graduated, that's when he wanted the divorce. So he gave me a list right before that. It said, "Here's what I expect of you, but I don't expect it all at once." But it was really a heavy-duty list. Take your time. So he came home from work that night and I handed him the list—it was all completed. I had bought a car, gotten my driver's license, lined up a job to start the following day and put down my last beer. No more drinks for me. I've had this happen a lot in my life where it's just never good enough. I mean, "Here's a list of what I want you to accomplish but I'm not expecting you to do it all in one day. Take your time." But then I did do it all in one day and when I said, "Hey could you grab me a Diet Coke out of the refrigerator?" he responded with, "You want another Diet Coke?" "No. No, as a matter of fact I don't."

It was constantly a battle. He really was the most adventurous human being I've ever known. People always asked why I would stay with such an abusive man. Well, I loved the adventure so much. Yes, that much! We went to the most beautiful exotic places. I loved it and I know it sounds terrible but I would take the beatings in exchange for that. Eventually it got to the point where the beatings were too much, though. I packed everything into my car that night including Peke-A-Boo and moved into town where I stayed with the homeless people.

So how did this keep happening? This cycle of abuse? Once again I saw myself as the rock on the river bank covered in moss. The rock that I'd become looked dry and colorless, sporting a green cloud overhead. As my luck would have it, someone came along and kicked me back into the river. This is where I hit rock bottom. I settled for this for a while until I realized I was surrounded by sludge. Once again the water was at my back, only this time it cleansed me. I felt like a fish, free to move around as I pleased. Wait a minute. What was that shiny thing in front of me? Oh no, I was hooked again. This being wanted to take my life. Well, since I knew it wasn't my time and I still had work to do here, I twisted, turned, and struggled to get free. This being had the hook in deep and really put up a fight to make me his possession.

This little fish story may sound silly, but when I reflect on the past, I find it easier to make such comparisons and bring a bit of lightness to the story. Being verbally or physically abused is just an ugly memory. Today I hop in and out of the river or sit on the side and dangle my feet. As I get a little older I like to be of the flow, not so sure I want to go with it anymore. It can get a little rough at times, not to mention it can also be a cold and lonely ride.

CHAPTER 18

On the Streets

I ended up in the state of Washington where I lived on the street for the next few months. Of my own choosing, mind you. I had no money and wasn't sure what my next move was going to be, and for now this seemed to be the best thing for me. I met the nicest people while I was living there. They could not have been kinder to me. Many were in a similar situation. Homeless people tend to get a negative rep, but the people I met chose to live that way for various reasons. They showed me the ropes. They were all super cool. I got food stamps and money and all kinds of stuff. I just survived. It was cold and it was raining, but the people were all so great. I was sleeping in my car. I hung out with the homeless crowd during the day in parks and in the marina and they were able to tell me a good place to park at night. I parked in a supermarket parking lot because I felt safe there and then I asked a couple of the other homeless people to pull up on the side of me just to guard me. Safety in numbers. Plus through everything, I had my Pekingese who stayed up all night and watched my back while I was sleeping. He only passed out in the morning when he saw me with my free cup of coffee from McDonald's. Once he knew I was good to go, he'd be on his back, sprawled out. Gotta get his rest, too! "I'm exhausted. You sure you're awake? Okay. Good night, Irene, I'm going down for the count!"

It was just an experience, you know? I don't even feel badly about it. It was just what happened. For bathrooms, there was always McDonald's and the market. On occasion I would go to the marina and sleep there. They not only had showers, but they also had laundry facilities. I was taught by the street people how you work the system and I learned well. When I was on food stamps, I could change them into money, which I needed for gas, paper goods, toiletries, etc. I could only eat so much food. There were other people who needed that food. You just made it work. I got smart. We would take the food to the park and cook it on one of the grills. They'd each give me a couple of bucks and that way it worked out for all of us.

Anyway, I was a street person for two full months and it was definitely better than my previous situation. That's for sure. However, it got to the point where I just couldn't live on the street any more. Even my sendoff was really very beautiful. When those guys shipped me out of Washington, it took me three whole days to get back home. The day that I was leaving, they all drove with me to the outskirts of town, filled my gas tank, and wished me a safe journey. Some of them were on motorcycles. So sweet. Here they were, these people, trying to make a little bit of money to survive every day but they escorted me to the state line when it was my time to go home. I had strapped my surfboard, my futon, and my tent to the top of my Chevy Cavalier station wagon (his name was Bob … after Marley, not anyone else). As I drove, the rope holding all my gear to the roof had started to loosen up. I began to hear this twittery flip-flop sound. I had just merged into a lane with a sign above it saying 405 South. I was in L.A. All of a sudden I heard a "Whoooosh!" I had one of those tents that you just throw into the air and they set themselves up. The damn thing suddenly flew off the back of my car and set itself up right in the middle of the busy freeway! Oh my God!

I guessed I was back.

PART V
FINDING
MY LIGHT

CHAPTER 19

My Way Back

I was in Los Angeles trying to figure out my next move
when I remembered a trailer park out in Valencia that I
had seen on many trips out of town. A great friend of the family
convinced me to check out an RV lot in the area. Said that might
be exactly what I was searching for. Off we went one early morning to find a home I could be comfortable in. I found a beautiful
one, but the money issue reared its ugly head. Once again I
found myself in a financial valley. This time I wasn't willing to
leave it up to a man. I would find another way, and I did. Marian
agreed to co-sign the loan for me so that I could move forward
with my plan. After that, and many thanks on my part, the RV
place also helped me with the lot where I could park my new
home.

The handling of this business transaction occurred inside
the sales office, but at one point I stepped outside because I
needed a cigarette. Out came the salesman, trying to hit on me.
Now I'd only been divorced a month, and after what I'd been
through, this was the last thing on my mind. After 10 minutes or
so of silly talk, he found the confidence to ask me out for a drink
sometime. It was kind of uncomfortable because I was still waiting for everything to go through on the loan and I didn't want to
mess that up.

"Oh sure," I said, having no real intention of ever going out
with this guy. "Just give me my trailer, dude," is what I really

wanted to say.

The day my trailer was delivered, I felt so free. Everything that was in it belonged to me. No men's underwear, no kids' toys, no skateboards—just me all settled in. Two days later, I realized that I needed to go to the market to stock the fridge. I stepped outside, shut the door, and realized that I didn't have a key to lock it. I'd never been given a set! I placed a call to the dealership and my original salesperson picked up the call.

"No problem," said Mark, the guy who had hit on me. "Is there anything else you'd like?"

I responded, "Yeah, a six-pack of beer."

Our first holiday together was Valentine's Day. The only thing I had left with my mother's writing on it was my birth certificate. Her handwriting was very unusual but when I opened his Valentine's card, the writing inside looked just like hers! It read, "I will always love you." In that second, all my dreams had come true. My mother had never really left me. I realized that she had guided the most wonderful father/brother/lover and friend into my life. The funniest thing, though, is that he never did bring me the keys!

I had been living in the trailer park for about two months and I was very happy. I'd only had about two weeks of the trailer to myself before Phonzo moved in with me. By that point, Chris was living with his girlfriend and Phonzo had been at Grandma's. Everyone was moving around quite a bit in those days. Life was good. Then one day a girl from the front office came to my trailer door via golf cart with a message that someone had called on the phone for me. She told me he'd be calling back on the pay phone up by the pool in 15 minutes. I had no idea who that might have been so I jumped in the car with her and waited by the phone until it finally rang. Oh my God. It was the second ex. He started by talking to me like we were the best of friends. He spoke mainly about all the great trips we'd been on and how we were "made for each other." People just didn't understand us, he added. I was absolutely speechless. I could not believe my own ears! When I wasn't giving him any feedback, he seemed to get nervous. That's when he started giggling to himself. He then cleared his throat and said, "You know, it's funny I just could not kill you." Wow. Just ... wow. Well, let me tell you it certainly wasn't for lack of trying! He just kept on laughing and I put the receiver down. That was the end. I've never heard from him or seen him ever again.

I've lived a pretty rocky road and I know it. If he could laugh that he couldn't kill me and I'm still here then I can still speak about it. That's the whole joke of it all. He laughed in my face that he couldn't kill me but God's got me so protected. I've got more work to do. That's my job here, to help other people, and there are still plenty of other people out there that need my help. I always try to put smiles on people's faces and that's what I'm going to keep on doing. That's who I am. I know it sounds so corny but, hey, what's wrong with being corny? I love corny! It's like watching that kid on *Leave It to Beaver* walking along with one foot on the curb and one on the street. My boyfriend Mark adores that scene because it reminds him of when things were innocent.

There isn't a day that I don't think of Peke-A-Boo. I can't overstress the importance of how much I love him still. There are pictures that go back from that time and you'd have a hard time finding one where we are not together. He just went every-where with me. One time, when I was living in my trailer, it was a very hot day. I had a doctor's appointment but I didn't know how long I was going to have to be there. I just couldn't take him with me. As I left the trailer, I closed the door on his little face. I had to push him back and tell him I couldn't take him this one time but I swear I could hear him saying, "That's it. I've had enough of you. Look! Oh, I almost fell! Now you're gonna feel bad if I hurt myself!" He stormed off back into the trailer SO mad! I started driving off but the guilt trip he had tried to give me worked. I thought, "Y'know what? Nothing is more important. I'm gonna turn around and go get him. And that's just what I did. When I got back, he was sitting at the front door with his lunchbox, his water bowl and his toys. "I knew you'd be back. Packed my stuff."

I said, "I love you."

CHAPTER 20

Missed Opportunity

I had a really good friend of mine who said, "You know, God gives you an opportunity to exit." I thought, "Wow that is so powerful." And he gave me one such opportunity. I was living in the trailer park. Mark had a severe case of psoriasis—it was all over his body really bad. We had been dating for only about six months and, of course, I had already been with him, touched him, seen him and all that, just like normal things that new couples do. I knew he was so uncomfortable with it. I just wanted to make him comfortable because everybody's got their own thing but Jesus, God almighty, did he ever get something horrific. So I finally asked him about it, but he didn't really want to discuss it.

He said, "I guess it has something to do with my liver."

"From drinking?" I asked.

"I guess. Whatever," he said. "Or an autoimmune disease."

I said, "Well, today we quit drinking!" We both decided that was a good idea for a lot of reasons. It just didn't have a place in our lives anymore. I can't recall ever a time in my life, or in anyone else's life, a story that ended with the line, "It's a good thing we drink." But there are plenty of disaster stories that end with the line, "Were you drinking?"

The next day, I was there in my trailer that I had purchased brand new six months earlier from Mark at the RV lot. That day, though, my air conditioning decided to quit working and it was, to put it mildly, hot. We were going through a 110-degree heat wave! Because we had both quit drinking, I noticed that I was feeling a little on the sleepy side in the late afternoon. I fell asleep on my bed for what I thought was just going to be maybe an hour nap but when I woke up, I was dehydrated. Now when you're dehydrated, your brain just goes south. It was a bad scene. There are a lot of people out there that when they get dehydrated they start hallucinating. That was me. It's up to you to decide if you believe what happened next. I'm just telling you what I saw from my side. The experience I'm about to relate to you restored a faith in God I was already pretty darn sure I had.

Here's where things got weird. I started having a hallucination. Are you ready for this? I woke up from that nap to find my tiny kitchen/dinette area filled with the most frightening real people! These characters could change their appearance in a second. They could go from looking almost preppy to the most demonic creatures you have ever seen! It didn't matter what form they were taking. Their sole—and I mean SOLE—purpose was to scare me and they were doing a good job. I was terrified!

The preppy group was screaming derogatory comments about me out the window of my trailer trying to humiliate me in front of my neighbors. In trailer parks, people tend to live more outside their units than inside. As trailer parks go, this one was state-of-the-art million-dollar units so my neighbors were not people with missing teeth and couches out on the front doorsteps, as people like to portray trailer parks. When the demons took over, their specialty was fear-based torturous games; the more fear they could inflict the funnier the games were to them. Through all the emotional bobbing and weaving of fear, I made a mistake that they could profit by.

Peke-A-Boo was lying on my bed. I made eye contact with him and showed that because I love him so much I was afraid for his safety right then. All this was just what they were looking for, something that I cared about. It's the same kind of mental torture that kidnappers do. Helplessness is a condition they love to put you in. They love to hurt you at the deepest core by hurting the ones you care about the most. It's a horrible feeling. Once I knew they were onto me, I got up from the dinette where I'd been sitting that whole time and pushed through them to my bedroom where I grabbed Peke-A-Boo.

I was just wearing my bathrobe and no shoes but once I had Peke-A-Boo in my arms, I ran out the door. The park was landscaped with white jagged pebbles and it housed about 1500 motorhomes, fifth wheels, trailers, and toy haulers, etc. Each was spaced 20 feet apart. I was so scared of these people and what I knew they were capable of—the changing of appearances and also the capability to change the landscape. I'm not talking about pebbles. I'm talking about moving buildings into places where there were none. Anything for them was possible! Except for one thing ... and I'll tell you what that was in a second.

Like in the scary movies, the person who is being chased is running (and usually falls, but in my case I didn't) and the person or persons doing the pursuing are slowly walking, as if to prolong your fear. Well, they were everywhere! Every turn I made, another would pop up. Just one big heart attack-type scare every other second. I even thought I saw people that I knew, friends of mine from the park, but it always turned out to be one of them. That's how creepy they could manipulate their appearances. After about five hours of this cat and mouse game, they trapped me down by the park's pool area. By this time they were all carrying nets and they had reconstructed the pool area into a torture chamber for Peke-A-Boo.

This chamber consisted of a noose hanging at the top of the slide which they planned to hook Peke-A-Boo up to and then push him down the slide leaving him to hang there while they gathered around to laugh at their masterpiece of sickness. I was standing right in the center of them, surrounded by the nets, and their continuous grabs at Peke-A-Boo trying to remove him from

my death grip. All of a sudden, I stared down one that I thought was the leader of the bunch. I explained to him that my love for Peke-A-Boo was of God and I would take his life myself as opposed to their humiliation and fear-based plan. The very mention of God stopped these creatures in their tracks. I looked him straight in his piercing eyes, as I put my arm around Peke-A-Boo's neck and started in to snap it while profusely professing my love for him. At that exact moment I must have collapsed. The hallucination was over.

A month later I woke up. Peke-A-Boo was alive, thank God! I had gone running around for five hours in my bare feet on the pebbles, so everybody says, and finally I just collapsed. In my body, every internal organ had shut down and I was just lying on the ground flopping around like a fish. Doctors told my family that it didn't look like I was going to make it and that if I did, I'd most likely never be the same. You have that happen to you once, you're not gonna be the same, that's for sure. You get into a car accident, you're not going to be the same. You'll always make sure now that the safety belt is on or make sure you don't tailgate. At that point, though, my vitals were off the charts and I was put into a medically induced coma to stabilize me. The kidneys would stabilize but not the liver, then the liver but not something else. It was like it kept bouncing around from organ to organ and the doctors kept chasing it!

I stayed in that hospital for a month. Mark, who had been at work when everything happened, visited two or three times a day for the entire month. Marian, my mother-in-law, said, "I've never seen anybody fight so hard to stay alive." Do you know why? I didn't want that opportunity. I wasn't ready. God gave me the opportunity and I could have done it right there. But I chose not to. I'm not quitting my job; I signed up for the long haul. I'll let you know when I'm ready to exit.

When I finally woke up, I did so in a room filled with bal-

loons, cards, flowers, and everything Pekingese! My fans had
sent beautiful messages of prayers and well wishes and I got this
big box of stuff. It was the most beautiful thing. Somebody had
gotten on the Internet and asked what I would like and my brother
said that I really loved my Pekingese. So they sent me everything
from calendars and coffee mugs to t-shirts and refrigerator mag-
nets, all with Pekingese dogs all over them! There were so many
letters from people saying, "We're praying for you," or "You
mean so much to us." Just the most lovely mail. It was all very
sweet and a belated big-time thank you goes to all of you who
took the time!

I had to relearn how to walk. It was unbelievable. My feet
were so abused from running on the pebbles. At one point, I
said, "I'm fine. I'll drive home." I promptly stood up and fell
right over. They sent a psychiatrist into my room.

The woman said, "Hi."

I said, "Hi."

"Can you do me a favor," she asked. I told her I wasn't even
sure if I could walk yet, but I'd give it a shot. I still had my sense
of humor. "Can you count backwards from 100 ... by 6's?" 94—
88—82 ... I looked at her for a second and then asked if she
could do it! Her response was to say, "I think this will be our last
meeting."

"Well, all righty then! Have a good day. Next!"

During my two weeks of recovery, I became a lime sherbet
junkie. I was depleting the hospital of lime sherbet. They started
telling me they didn't have any more.

"You ate it all."

"Can you order some? I want some more!" Good friends of
mine had come in while I was still in the coma. One brought a
boom box to play reggae music. That's my favorite type of music.
Other friends would come in and just massage me or talk to me
and it was really cool.

As expected, the only person who wasn't cool was my first

163

ex-husband who brought my children to see me while I wasn't a pretty sight. I'm sure I was all purple and swollen and ugly. I really don't know what I looked like but people have told me. I was sad for my kids to have to see me, but it was worse when their dad said, "I told you she'd wind up like this."

I'm well aware that dehydration played a major role in my ordeal. My status when I arrived at the hospital was nonetheless bleak. All my internal organs had shut down. My doctor's diagnosis on a daily basis was that he didn't think I was going to make it. But I did.

Okay so now on to the alcohol period. There were not too many hours during any given day you could catch me without a drink in my hand. I pretty much started out drinking beer with an occasional margarita or other mixed girly drinks. One stretch of time, I only drank champagne. It was part of my Marilyn Monroe period. When I first moved to the beach I quit drinking for over a year, but started up again because of the company I was keeping. No one forced me, of course. It was just easier to blend in at the time. It was no fun to be sober amongst intoxicated companions. In the past, when I was in my 20s, I played around with cocaine for a while. I even freebased a couple of times. I was experimenting like a lot of others in the crowd I hung around with. Fortunately, narcotics just never seemed to grab hold of me. I don't think I ever paid for any of that stuff. I did, however, smoke pot quite frequently. I pretty much could take it or leave it, though.

Before I ever started drinking, I used to have this crazy addiction to 7/11 stores! Back then, a Big Gulp was an extension of my hand. I love Diet Coke and had to have it 24/7. When I was a kid, I used to suck my thumb. It was that hand-to-mouth thing. I'm back on Diet Coke again now. It's just too bad that I couldn't have skipped the whole alcohol phase. The alcohol had imprisoned me. I could think of nothing else and even found

that I was becoming a hermit. I wouldn't leave the house unless my next destination was another source of wine. Wine was my last favorite drink of choice before I quit. I used to drink it in a Big Gulp cup and it had to be chock-a-block full of ice. Chardonnay was my favorite.

I will tell you I've been smoking cigarettes since I was about 12! Like a lot of other people, I thought it looked cool. I remember one wardrobe lady on the set of *Land of the Lost* who had long acrylic nails and those slim, brown Sherman cigarettes. I used to steal maybe a cigarette or two a week on the set. I wonder if she ever noticed. Behind the stage there were bungalows with bathrooms inside. That's where I would sneak off to smoke my stolen cigs. In the bathroom was a big mirror. There I would stand with paperclips stuck to my fingernails pretending they were fake acrylics while I waved my cigarette around talking to myself in the mirror. I thought I was the shit.

Now it's just the opposite. Quitting smoking is next on my bucket list. I really need to get to the place in my head where I can just put them down and walk away from them as I have done with the alcohol, and have no withdrawal or desire to have it in my life anymore. I'll get there. The habit is becoming more and more a pain in the neck. I feel it stealing time from me that otherwise could be spent having truly fun moments.

CHAPTER 21

Wilt the Stilt

*I*n my "Really Lost Days," as I now call them, I had many sexual partners; often it was because I really wanted somebody to hold me, and you had to put out in order to get that. Sad to say that I did because I was stupid. I just wish somebody could have hugged me. But you know what? I can tell you from experience that a lot of people really suck at sex! And I don't mean literally. I mean they just are really bad. They don't even get what it's all about. They're either doing it too fast or they're going the wrong way. God, slow your roll. It's amazing to think what some people consider lovemaking to be. I've been with really good-looking guys and rich ones, really famous ones … and they're usually horrible.

Wilt Chamberlain. Wilt the Stilt claimed to have done the deed with more than 20,000 women in his lifetime. I was not one of them. I was at the Rainbow again, where I had met Tony, when I met Wilt some time later. I've seen Gene Simmons and Paul Stanley, Bret Michaels … you see rock and rollers there every time you hang and that was my local spot for a while. I lived right down the street so I'd go there two or three times a week. One night, there was a big tall guy there in the Rainbow. I'm not just talking taller than I am, mind you. This guy was a giant! I met him in the upstairs. The upstairs of the place was called Over the Rainbow and it was an exclusive club. You had to pay to get into the upstairs, or if you were cute they'd let you go up for free.

So I was up there and there was this big, giant guy. Now I come from a family of tall people. All of my brothers are at least 6' or above and my sisters and I are all 5'8" which, years ago, used to be considered tall for women. Nowadays, a model has to be at least 6' tall.

I had this kind of tall complex thing so I went up to him and said, "Jesus, how tall are you?"

He said, 7' 2" and asked me my name.

I said, "I'm Kathleen."

"Nice to meet you, Kathleen. My name's Norman."

Turns out it was Wilt Chamberlain, probably the most recognizable basketball player in the country back then. It seems his middle name was Norman. He asked what I did for a living. I told him I used to be on a TV show, *Land of the Lost*. "I'm sure you don't know it," I said.

"You're right," was his response.

I said, "Okay, 'Norman, we're gonna have a bet here. I'm gonna bet you more people who come up these stairs right here know who I am than know who you are and whoever loses has to buy the other person breakfast." I was confident I'd win and I did, because the crowd there was more my age group. Of course, if you have any intelligence, Wilt outclasses me a billion kazillion times, but it was just some stoners there. We heard, "Wilt who?" a lot that night. Hah! So he lost, and in order to come with me to buy me breakfast, he had to get into the back of my car, which was still that Toyota Tercel. If you remember, the back of a Tercel looked like an ATM machine. It looked like if you stuck a credit card in there you could get 20 bucks out of it. So Wilt was curled up in the backseat. How in the world he got in there, I have no idea. But I had some 8 by 10s of myself lying around in the back of the car for interviews and one of them was of me in a bikini. He started doing the naughty in the back seat of my car! Again, I swear to Christ I never had sex with the man, although I know he had that reputation. I played tennis with him and we did lunches and talked on the phone for hours and hours all the time but never that. Not that he didn't try.

One night, for instance, I had had a particular bummer of a day so I called him and said. "Wilt, I just need some company." He told me to come on up to his house. Now, I'd never been to his house before but, like most people, I had read that he had a bedspread that had the faces of 12,000 Arctic wolves on it, all stitched together. He really did. I saw it! Prior to reaching his house—coincidentally located in Bel Air—there was an intercom box that you had to punch; they could see you and know who's waiting at the gate. So I drove up and hit the box … only it wasn't Wilt. It was, of all people, my old "nemesis," Farrah Fawcett, whose weight Mum had always brought up to me! How weird was that?

"Wilt's next door," she said very sweetly.

I simply said, "Oh, I'm sorry." Then I had to back out. Once I finally ended up in the right place, the next thing I knew, he was trying to do the freaky thing with me. I told him, "No, no, no, that isn't gonna happen. That's not what I came up here for!" And it never ever happened between us. This book is all about truth and the truth is, it never did happen. But we stayed good friends and we spoke often right up until he passed.

C H A P T E R   2 2

The Sally

I've had more than my share of situations I'd like to forget but there's one for which I would have an easier time doing so if only I could understand how I wound up in the situation to begin with. From what I can remember it began with a little group I had joined. It was headed by another former child actor who had appointed himself to the position. In fact, its congregation was an ensemble of ex-childhood stars who had taken a wrong path or two. I attended a few of the group gatherings, and at first they seemed pretty harmless. Most kid actors have very similar stories to tell so the meetings always had plenty of laughter and compassion to go around.

Meanwhile, my boys were both adults by then and had been staying with their father off and on. There was quite a bit of substance abuse going on at Bob's apartment, but at the time I was a beer chugger and that was pretty much it. One day, however, when I was at his apartment, I was passed a pipe load of chronic and teased and dared to snap it. I recall the smoke going down my throat but what followed was a mad dash to the bathroom. I didn't even make it to the toilet. The shower door was open and blocking the seat, so that's where I unloaded my sickness. Yuck! I somehow wound up on the couch and could hear people laughing and saying something about "Global Death." Apparently this was the name of the strain of herb I had just ingested. As I drifted off, I remember thinking, "Yeah. Very funny, motherfu..."

When I woke up, I was no longer on that couch. I was in a hospital bed and there was blood all underneath me. Ten days I stayed in that room. I had daily doctor visits but no diagnosis of what was wrong with me. Twenty diaper changes a day had become normal. On the tenth day I finally was diagnosed with what they hesitantly called a "super infection."

That same day my mother-in-law Marian showed up at the hospital, along with the ringmaster of that ex-childhood actors' circus. Between the two of them, they had come up with this holier than thou, "We're going to save her," intervention-type plan. I was wheeled to the hospital pharmacy, handed some pills, given a plastic bag with some clothing in it and taken by the ringmaster to the Salvation Army facility in downtown L.A. I still wasn't sure what was going on. Do you have any idea how gnarly that was? It was Christmas time and I was dumped off there with only a box of diapers and that plastic bag of clothes (which contained an old robe, a mismatched belt and a pair of old lady red slippers). The women who ran that facility looked like the hardest core lesbians you've ever seen. I felt so violated by their stares after they checked me in. Mind you, I literally had no idea why I was there.

They put me in a room with three other girls. One of those girls had so many open sores on her body that I thought she was just going to explode and, by God, they all wanted me to take a shower first thing! I clung to my robe for dear life. I was eventually given a schedule of the day's events—meal hours, free time in the group area, smoking times, etc. The group area was where the phone was. Over the course of a few days, I found that the $10 bill that my mother-in-law had apparently given me was absolutely of no use in that place. You had to have change for the vending machines and everyone hung on to their change like grim death. In order to go into the room where the free time took place, you had to have real shoes. So my slippers and I were confined to my room. In the evening, we were put in single file and marched across the street to The Sally. "The Sally" is what they call these Salvation Army places. We were instructed not to talk to any of the men. Unbeknownst to me, these guys would be serving our meals to us. Well, for God's sake, I made the mistake of saying thank you for my tray of food. I was yanked out of the line and told that my phone privileges would be removed for my "outburst."

I wasn't allowed in that phone room anyway. So I sat by myself that night eating the worst garbage you can imagine. That was it. I wasn't speaking to anyone after that, not even those human bulldozers that ran the joint. Days went by, pills were popped, diapers were changed and putrid food went down my gullet. All that sulking I did finally paid off. I was allowed a cigarette break and free time, slippers and all. One day the main bulldozer, who wasn't too happy with me, made the mistake of saying, "You know you don't have to be here. We're doing *you* a favor getting you clean and all." When my ears got wind of this I made a beeline for the gated front door, pushed on the buzzer frantically and ran straight out and smack into Skid Row. Cardboard boxes along the street, trashcan fires, the whole nine yards.

I remember that it was raining, I was in my robe and slipper ensemble, and I was horrified and mumbling to anyone who would listen, "Where's the bus?" Somebody finally pointed up the street and I just started running. The last thing I saw before I jumped on that bus was a man at the bus stop wearing baseball gloves for shoes. I was in a complete state of shock. I was shaking like a leaf. A black woman in business attire stopped me, tapped me on the shoulder and asked me if I knew where I was headed. I had no clue. I must've muttered Culver City, Bob's neighborhood. She said she would sit with me until that stop and let me know where to get off. From the bus, I managed to find my way to a donut shop. I asked the guy behind the counter to call the only phone number I could come up with. It turned out to be my son Phonzo's number. I found out later that Phonzo caught whatever I originally had, too, although apparently not to the same degree. He came for me and got me home safely. Why this whole fiasco happened to me leaves my head shaking to this very day!

What a freaking nightmare!

PART VI
LOST
LESSONS

CHAPTER 23

Slowly I Return

*I*n the early 2000s, the *Land of the Lost* DVDs started coming out from Rhino Entertainment and there I was. It was the first time I'd appeared before the public in any way for quite a while. I didn't want to get on the screwed-up-child-actor-on-drugs daytime talk show circuit. Rhino found me somehow and asked me if I would do some episode commentaries. In exchange, they gave me a couple grand. I was basically broke and I just jumped up and said, "Oh, yeah!" Should have probably signed a better contract. What I should have done was held out for a percentage of sales but, hey, desperate people do desperate things. I had been so wealthy in my life and at that time I was not. Well, I'm actually very wealthy in my life as far as all that good stuff you can't buy with money. Sometimes I'm really rich and sometimes $100 looks great. It goes like that in my life. It does for everybody, but people think that just because you did a series once, you're still rich. That just doesn't happen. And I'm okay with that.

The commentaries were recorded in Howard Hughes' vault! It was a bank in Hollywood that used to actually belong to Hughes and the rooms were set up with microphones and headsets and God knows whatever other tech gadgets. Rhino came out with a four-episode set first and I did an on-camera interview for that. Then they came out with the full seasons where we all did commentary for a couple episodes and I did another interview.

Wesley, Phil, and I were asked to watch the shows and give our commentary to be included with the box set. We had a great time watching and talking and reminiscing. Hopefully you've had a chance to see them because you can tell we were having fun! Phil really is tenderhearted. He's very uptight in some ways, but very sweet, too. When I start talking to him, though, even now, he gets giddy like he's 10 years old again. He's just adorable. On the DVD interviews, you can hear us giggling. We just couldn't stop. It's truly how we roll.

After we finished recording, Wesley and I were standing outside and our competitive nature came back just like it had been during filming all those years ago. He turned to me and said, "How come you got a limousine? I didn't get a limousine!" Then he jumped into the kind of average car that was provided for him. Before he left, however, we told each other how much we meant to each other and how much we loved each other. It was so very nice. We really had a good time working on those DVD commentaries. We couldn't stop cracking up. I'm sure they edited some of the swearing—some of our more private moments. After all, kids will be watching these DVDs with their families!

Of course I was just a kid when the show filmed so my job was really to follow direction. I showed up on time, said what I was told to say, jumped on what I was told to jump on, rode something, ran through some bushes, went to school, got up and did the same thing again the next day. A while back, I watched an episode on DVD that I had not seen in over 35 years. The actual disc has a picture of Wesley on it and I think it's the first episode of the third season. I was like, wow! I really did a good job! I was actually impressed with myself. Much of that stuff on the show seems cheesy now, but there are times when I think I did really well. There's one scene where I kept floating in and

Run, Holly, Run!

out of my own self. I wasn't in the red shirt and the burgundy
corduroys. I had a yellow shirt and tan pants and I didn't have
calves. I only had knees. I watched it with some friends and I
couldn't help thinking, *I was good as me!*

CHAPTER 24

Marshall(s)

After the DVD experience went so well, I was ready to get back in the public eye and do what I do best—entertain. But there was one problem. To make ends meet I had been working at Marshall's department store and hating it (although looking back on it I did have pretty good insurance). We called it "Holly Marshall's." Kind of funny, I know. Ha ha. Holly Marshall. Come on now. It beat the hell out of Del Taco where I had been previously.

Mark had encouraged me get a job not only to be a contributor but also, I guess, just to keep me busy. Peke-A-Boo was suffering greatly at that time. He was left alone too much and was not used to that type of solitude. He passed on about six months into that job. Marshall's was also where I was working when I lost Al and Marian, my in-laws. Just so many memories of that whole time. Three pretty big blows for me.

Try to explain to your boss why you have to keep missing work. I know he thought I was lying. I kept having to bring him newspaper clippings. I told him my mother had died and I wasn't going to be able to come in that day. Somebody else in the store apparently said, "You know what? She is lying because her mother died 20 years ago." But do you know what? I was "adopted" by another mother with the same name, just a different spelling. I got to have each one for about 25 years. That wasn't a lie.

Run, Holly, Run!

As much as I hated working at those places, it was a good experience for me and I'll tell you why. When I got in there, for the first few days, I thought for the life of me I am never going to learn how to do that stuff. You want me to sing a song? That I can do. Tap dance? Start the music. I could not, however, get the hang of pushing all those buttons and having a headset on while at the same time starting to serve food. "I'm never gonna get this!" I kept telling myself. But every day I asked one fewer question and you know what? I actually conquered it eventually and I was very good. At both Del Taco and Marshall's. It was something I proved to myself. If the shit hits the fan and I have to do that, I actually can! That made me feel good about myself. Maybe making my own money and being responsible wasn't so scary after all.

In fact, some other good things came out of that experience. One night when I came home from my shift, Mark greeted me with a suggestion. "Why don't you write a book?" It would take some time and it wouldn't pay the bills right then, but he always looks at the big picture. I was so happy to quit, and writing a book seemed like a dream come true. In the beginning I was diligently writing chapters every day. In the evenings, when Mark came home from work, we sat in front of the fireplace and I read to him what I had written that day. I was very excited. I was really into it for a time, but I think I got writer's block. A lot of the papers that I wrote had blurred marks from where I was crying. I liked it when I could make it a story. I wanted it to flow like a nice wave. That might have been a low spot in the valley but there were mountains that I got up on, too, and everything looked beautiful from up there. I'm not being a crybaby. I don't want sympathy. It's not about that. Now, compassion I'll take all day long. I have had such a glorious life, really—good, bad, and otherwise. I think it's cool that I survived all this shit! So Mark would listen patiently every night, but then he began to tell me how he would've written my story. That didn't go over very well with me, of course.

He said, "I don't like what you wrote today."

"What are you talking about?"

He said, "I think you should write …."

I told him, "That's not the way it happened. I'm writing the way it happened, okay? If you wanna write your own book, maybe you can write one about me! I don't even give a shit. But don't tell me how to write my book. Without the truth, what's the point of me even doing it?"

He wouldn't shut up about it, though, and about a month into this routine, after many of my own snappy comebacks, I finally lost it. I told him to shut up and then I swung my hand with a pen in it and poked him in the arm. I got him pretty good, I guess. It was bleeding and he was screaming and I ended up getting arrested on a domestic violence charge. I don't think it was worthy of having me arrested, but he did. There wasn't really that much blood but he spread it around to look worse at the time because he was so mad. He practically painted himself with it to make it look bad

I spent three whole days in jail. I'd never been in trouble *like that* before in my entire life and I was scared to death the whole time. It was all one big freaky nightmare. They took me to this tiny cell with a lot of other girls in there.

"I can't go in there," I said.

The guard said, "There's a bigger one downtown."

"Oh, no, this will be fine."

The girls started telling me, "Here's what's gonna happen." They all knew the routine and I'd never been arrested in my life so I didn't even know the correct terms. I had no idea what to expect. They said, "First you're gonna have your PD—Public Defender—then you're gonna have a DA—District Attorney—then you're gonna have an arraignment."

I said, "Where do they put that?" I thought all these things were examinations of some sort and because I had given birth I

Run, Holly, Run!

could probably handle it. That's how ignorant I was of the jail system. It was just something I'd never done before. One of my cellmates was a heroin addict so, of course, my luck, when we headed out for the courthouse I got chained to her. The other girls were smart, though, because they were professional go-to-jail people. They knew the routine.

As we marched, my partner kept falling over and hurting my arm and I hollered, "Get up! I'm not dragging you." So then we got in the courtroom and one woman told me whatever I did, not to cry. The judge didn't like crying, she said. "Whatever you do, don't look at your boyfriend if he happens to be in the audience because it'll probably make you cry." So I was standing there and when it came my turn to step up and walk over there, believe it or not, one of the lawyers—the PD—asked me for my autograph! Jeez. Was he crazy? That was absolutely the last thing I needed to have happen at that moment. Up until that point my secret had been safe. Nobody knew who the hell I was. He wasn't my PD at least, but it was just very surreal and, looking back, pretty funny.

Mark was sitting there in the courtroom, dressed to the nines, and I did look at him. He's a very handsome man. He looks a lot like Craig Ferguson, or to be more precise, a combination of Harrison Ford and Craig Ferguson with a little David Bowie thrown in. He had on a great suit.

He stood up and said, "Your Honor, may I address the court?" Kind of weird. Nobody ever stands up in the audience.

The judge said, "Now just who the hell are you?"

Mark pleaded my case, "This is a really good woman, Your Honor. This has all been blown way out of proportion."

The judge started to say, "I'm gonna give you ..." and paused. I almost collapsed! I had been in the jail for 3 days—no sleep, no food. And I was thinking, *this is gonna kill me!* Then after a long minute he finished by telling me my sentence was to attend a year-long class on domestic violence.

181

So that's what I did. I completed all the classes. It took me a year and a half to actually finish them. On my graduation day, my teacher asked me if I wouldn't mind filling in for him that day because he had to attend an unexpected appointment. Then I went in the following week and I handed my papers to the judge. I was standing there and the PD put his arm around me. Good grief! So damn funny. He had his arm around me!

The judge said, "Okay, it's all good. Everything is done."

I said, "Your honor, would you mind? I know I'm not allowed to approach your bench, but do you mind if I give you a long distance handshake for being so nice to me through all of this?"

He said no and then he paused and I thought *uh-oh, I'm in trouble*. He didn't look at all pleased. I was afraid for a minute there that he was going to have me put back in the pokey or make me take another class.

"No," he said, "but I will allow my bailiff to escort you up to my chair." How lovely was that? I walked up past all the other people, who were mostly traffic violators that day.

The judge put out his hand and I shook it and I looked him straight in the eye and said quietly, "I hope I never see you again."

As I was leaving he yelled out to me, "Finish your book!"

CHAPTER 25

Comic-Cons

*W*hen the Internet came along, there were all of these fan sites wondering whatever happened to the *Land of the Lost* stars. At that time no one had any idea where I was until I did that commentary on the DVD set. In a very strange way that longtime absence actually worked to my benefit because now, when I do shows or personal appearances, people are really excited. They may have seen the other celebrity guests over and over again but they hadn't seen me in a long time so that has actually worked in my favor.

So I began doing personal appearances and fans loved it! It was definitely a learning curve for me because this was a whole new animal. I was back in front of people who couldn't wait to hear my stories about the show and my life. I mean, they knew way more than I did about a lot of the technical stuff so I was learning right along with them. I can say that I've really gained an affinity for these die-hard fans and I do my best to make sure their experience is the best it can be.

I put my "oneness technique" into practice quite a bit at these shows. I have found that the people who attend these events view them as a family get-together. I believe some in attendance use these annual events much like we think of Thanksgiving or Christmas as a time with our families. It's a time for them to see celebrities and attendees that they connect with. So when someone approaches my table I put this oneness into high gear.

I usually let them know that I've been on both sides of the table. This seems to make them feel relaxed knowing that I can be a fan just like them. I let them ask me all the standard *LOTL* questions:

What was it like wearing the same clothes?
Were you afraid of the Sleestaks?
Do you still hang out with the cast?
How old were you when the show started?
Did you like the Will Farrell movie?

It goes on and on, but you get the picture. Maybe you're one of the people who has asked me those questions! After this conversation has taken place, I usually tell them to ask me a question that they will truly remember, something really special. And I do my best to answer it. I also ask them questions about their lives because it all fascinates me. Then we may take photos and I make sure to put their arms around me, even if they are a bit shy or hesitant. Sometimes they are just not sure what is okay and what isn't, so I take the lead. Who wants a picture with me with your hands down by your side? Oh, no. That doesn't make for a very memorable picture.

Nobody ever leaves my table without a big smile on their face. I've even shed a few tears with some. It can be a very emotional experience. Their stories can be so touching. It makes me feel good that later, after the show is done, I'll see posts on social media saying what a good time they had meeting me. That's what oneness is all about.

There have been some very interesting experiences at these shows. Let me tell you about a few of them:

One time a man approached my table. He showed me a picture of one of the original Sleestak costumes. He had purchased it at a Krofft auction. Well, I had never seen one of those costumes that didn't have a person in it. This photo showed it splayed out on the floor, flat as a board. It looked like E.T. when he was sick

and dying. I actually gasped at the photo. A dead Sleestak was very disturbing. Fans always ask if I was afraid of those Sleestaks because they were scared as hell when they watched at home as kids, sitting cross-legged on the floor. I always say no. The costumes were made out of wetsuit material and around the set, the actors wore them pulled down to their waist like surfers do. So I was used to them, but that deflated Sleestak he showed me was another story.

One of the coolest things happened when I was sitting with ... well, no names but a whole crew of older "former stars" in Atlanta, at Dragon Con. A very attractive woman stood up and said, "I don't have a question. I just have a statement. If it weren't for you, I wouldn't be the woman that I am today." Awwww! I almost collapsed on that one. Then she comes up to me and whispers, "*You* actually look really good." Ha ha ha! I thought that was the coolest thing.

People attend those shows and celebrities agree to them for many different reasons. When they rolled up Soupy Sales in a wheelchair, I was thinking, "Oh, now that is just too much." I was so mad at the people that were wheeling him up next to me. Then I found out that it wasn't them forcing him to do all that. He wanted his fans to have what might well be one last glimpse. So I stood back on that one. He was on an oxygen tank and really looked weak. Everyone was standing around him making this great big fuss. My first thought was, "Can't you just leave him alone? Can't you see that he's sick?" But Soupy had been in the business for so long that he had that understanding of fans that I didn't yet have. He had a wicked, wild career and he kept giving right to the end.

At another convention that I was working, the Teenage Mutant Ninja Turtles were there and a volunteer who was sitting next to me at my table mentioned that her granddaughters were big fans but that money was a little tight for her at the time. So I went over and traded some of my photos to the Turtles and came back with autographs for the kids. The Turtles were happy. They liked *Land of the Lost*. The lady was thrilled. And you know what? I felt pretty darn good, too.

I snuggled up to a lady fan in the audience at a Dragon Con and we watched "Elsewhen" together. She said, "This is my favorite episode."

I said, "Mine, too. Be quiet, we're watching it."

She went on to say, "I just in a million years never thought one day I'd be sitting next to you," and here I was all cuddled up like an egg in her lap.

"Ain't life a gas?" I said to her. Those moments. That's what I live for.

For me, it's really fun to be a celebrity again for a few moments every now and then. There's a responsibility in that and I like having the power again so that I can do something: not the power of being a celeb, but the power that comes with it that lets you get to do things that in your day-to-day life you may not ever be able to do. It always feels like it's my birthday. You're allowed to get away with stuff when you're a celebrity. But for me on those days, I take advantage of that in a different way. Whatever I get away with anymore is only so that I can do something for someone else.

I believe in the magic. *Land of the Lost* was a kids' television show on Saturday mornings so many years ago now. More than four decades ago! We were basically a babysitter for parents. Why has it hung on this long? Magic! The other part of that are all the fans I meet when I'm on the road and how it touched them. I constantly hear, "You were my first crush." I hear that all the time! You have to put yourself in that time and space and these little boys were about eight or nine and they just had a crush on me, you know?

How adorable is that?

CHAPTER 26

Reconnecting with the Cast

*W*hile I get a great reaction from fans, it's even more exciting when the cast is together. Wesley and I do most of the shows and it's been like a renewal of our relationship. Forty some odd years and it continues to blossom. Back when we were filming I always felt very comfortable around him. Although he was an adult, he never treated me like a kid. We used to horse around, sometimes even while filming. He would get a certain look in his eyes and I knew mischief was on its way. There was a large gap of time between the show ending and our involvement in the conventions.

Most of my adult life I just had contact with him through phone lines. These conversations were basically check-ins to see if all was well, nothing too deep. These last five years is when our relationship took off. If I only had known how easy it is to talk to him in regard to anything, I would have never have let so much time go by. Not only is he understanding in all aspects of life, but he's extremely intelligent, and off the wall when it comes to his sense of humor. When we are all together, we never stop laughing.

As far as shows go we are a well-oiled machine. It's almost telepathic the way we can communicate via thoughts. We put on a big display at these shows and give the fans 100 percent of our energy. If you were to ask someone who has stepped up to our booth what kind of experience they had, even 100 percent might sound a little low. Most of the time these comic-con events provide us with airfare, hotel, and a per diem, but once in a while, if it's a Los Angeles-area show, they get us our own hotel rooms. To save a little money, if it's a small show, we stay together in the same suite.

You know, when I was 12, I didn't really think too much about people's sexuality. I loved boys, the *Tiger Beat* kind, probably because they were unattainable, no sex stuff. Just posters and little girl dreams. I could live off a kiss like the one from Leif for months on end. So I guess when I heard that Wesley was gay, I already loved him as a person. I was still very young and my mind wasn't developed enough to understand why some people don't like that. Plus, in the Hollywood crowd, after I found out he was gay I was hard pressed to find someone who wasn't. Another thing, Wesley was very private and never discussed his personal business in front of anyone. He had not come out publically during the show. To put it simply, it wasn't the subject of the day. Nobody cared. I'll tell you something funny. Mum used to use the word "gay" around the house and it meant "happy." So was Wesley happy? Damn right!

So anyway, these days Wesley, his partner Richard, and I often bunk together as Richard will sometimes play the Sleestak character at the conventions. It's like a big slumber party. The activities of any such evening can include theatre productions, lots of singing and dancing, joke telling, and any other crazy thing we can dream up. One night in New Jersey at the Chiller Convention, we all stripped off our shirts (even Phil Paley was with us) and jumped under the covers with two Sleestak heads, all of us covered up to our chests. Looking very conspicuous. Our agent was in the room with us and photographed the whole scene. We posted it on Facebook so our fans could have a laugh as well. I frequently post photos on Facebook. I like to keep the fans abreast of what's new in my life and any news regarding *LOTL*. I even post old family photos to make them feel that they are really included.

I've mentioned all the laughter Wesley and I share. Just like anyone else, we go through some pretty rough times, too. Many tears have been shed between the two of us. Needless to say, but I'll say it anyway, I love Wesley! He's as much of a brother to me as he is a wonderful and true friend. Did I say how talented he is? Impersonations are his specialty; not anyone in particular, but just character types. Over the past few years I've been introduced to many of his friends and every single one of them is an absolute joy. A true reflection of who he is.

His partner Richard (the Sleestak) is such a wonderful addition to the *LOTL* crew. He adds his special touch at the shows and people really get a kick out of him. As a person, you couldn't ask for a more well-rounded being. Funny, smart, easy-going and caring. Wesley says he finally found the love of his life. Which works for me; I love him, too. So for all of you out there who wonder if I stay in touch with the cast, well, one down two to go.

On the surface, we couldn't be more opposite. Phil Paley is so clean-cut, extremely organized, and very meticulous. On the other hand, I'm one sidewalk away from Haight-Ashbury. I'm petty organized and only meticulous in certain areas, whereas Phil has perfect handwriting (mostly printing) and his apartment is decorated in Feng Shui. Everything is pointed in the proper direction, even down to the keys to his car, which can be found on the countertop in his kitchen pointed due west.

When Phil was growing up, his family had two little Shih Tzu dogs. So his introduction to the group was instilled at a young age. This brings up one of our strong bonds. Peke-A-Boo Jones got under Phil's skin and into his heart just like he did everyone else's. When Phil was in his mid-twenties he lived with me for a while. We had dated a few years prior, but this was round two. We were no longer dating, but nonetheless we were still super close. Every night Phil asked if Peke-A-Boo could sleep with him. I always checked on Phil out in the living room and the two of them were a couple of snuggle bunnies. This whole bond thing developed into its own language. Peke-A-Boo had more nicknames customized for his body parts. Like for instance, his front feet were referred to as Puttie Paws. His hind legs were another story.

When I was little, Mum had a friend named Dottie Marsh. Dottie used to babysit me, and she had the most unusually shaped legs. So all through my childhood anyone who had unique-looking legs was referred to as Dottie Marsh. And that's what Pekingese back legs are like. Sometimes we'd cut it short—Marshes, Dotties, etc.

One thing Phil and I love to do together is laugh. And I know what it takes to bring him into a state of absolute silliness. He's a very bright guy and very driven. He put himself through college at UCLA and proceeded to his current position as a legal technical advisor. He dissects laptops, cellphones, and the like as evidence for legal cases. When it came down to either Phil or Moosie being cast as Cha-Ka, I'm glad in the end it was Phil. Moosie had so many more experiences already. Phil has really adopted the character whole-heartedly. He is Cha-Ka. A handsome one at that. A lot of people thought it was Clint Howard under the mask. I think it was the eye color and the forehead that gave that impression and started the urban legend.

Like Wesley, Phil and I share telepathic type of communication. We are just one big, happy family. I know that is hard to believe because so many actors on shows don't get along. That's not the case with us. Honest.

Of course I can't leave out Spencer. I wouldn't dare. I told you we reconnected once, briefly when I was 18, but much later we had a very interesting encounter. You'll see what I mean when you get to the Epilogue at the end!

CHAPTER 27

Remakes Make Me Nauseous

I always thought that *Land of the Lost* would make a fantastic big budget adventure movie. Back in the late '90s, I remember Sid and Marty had a handshake deal or something to do a big screen version with Sony Pictures, but that never happened and Universal ended up with the rights. With every other old TV series from *The Addams Family* to *Bewitched* being dragged out and made into a feature film, I figured it was just a matter of time. There was a movie called *Journey to the Center of the Earth*. They had a T-Rex in it but I knew it could never have the magic that a *Land of the Lost* movie would have. *Journey* would come and go and be on DVD in a few weeks. A *Land of the Lost* movie, though, would be huge. Sid is the magic behind *Land of the Lost* and he wanted to see it happen, too. He said to me, "You have no idea." But I really did, because I believe in the magic. But time just kept racing ahead and next thing you know I had spent more than 30 years waiting for that damn phone to ring. Then came the day that it finally did.

I always screen my phone calls but when I heard, "This is Rachel, Brad Silberling's associate on the movie, *Land of the Lost*," I swear to Christ, I dove right across my desk. I'd been waiting for that call forever and it finally came through. And then I did this silly little dance all over the apartment. It was the dumbest dance ever, but I couldn't have cared less. My dream had finally come to fruition. Or so it seemed.

The *Land of the Lost* movie starred Will Ferrell as Rick Marshall. The new Holly was not a girl at all but a young adult, played by a brunette actress from Great Britain named Anna Friel. She was playing a character named Holly but she was not playing Holly Marshall. She was Rick Marshall's girlfriend! The Will character wasn't her brother, either. He was just a small-time con man and a tour guide. Still, in spite of the changes, Sid and Marty were involved in it so I was confident that they'd make sure it didn't get screwed up.

After shooting got underway, Mark and I drove down to visit the set at Universal. I was so excited on many levels. When Mark first met me, he had never seen *Land of the Lost* or any of the other things I'd done so it was kind of fun to show him all this stuff that had once been my world. Only if Mark behaves himself am I able to relax. He tends to say the wrong things to the wrong people unintentionally. For instance, when he was introduced to Billie Hayes (*HR Pufnstuf*'s Witchiepoo) at the *TV Land Awards* we attended together, he said, "It's very nice to meet you, Sir." Mind you, she does dress pretty butch, sort of like Chaz Bono gear, and her name is "Billie," but nonetheless it was uncomfortable all around. You see what I mean? Mark needs a short leash. He means well. It's just ignorance—and I say that kindly—when it comes to the show biz part of my life.

When we arrived on the lot, we were directed to the areas related to where *Land of the Lost* was shooting. The production had taken up five whole soundstages on the Universal lot for interiors and as we drove by them we were waved down by the movie's director, Brad Silberling. I was really excited at the time. As Mark pulled up, I asked Brad where we should park. He said to go ahead and just park right there. He then escorted us to Soundstage 27 where we were able to catch the filming of Marshall and Will in one of the opening scenes of the film.

At the time, I wasn't really aware of the strategy of the movie. I was well aware that this was a film version and that

Run, Holly, Run!

over 30 years had passed, but, after spending the afternoon observing, I just couldn't seem to get a handle on where they were going with the thing. I knew the fans were going to be confused, though, when Anna Friel kissed Rick Marshall! Well that couldn't have been me! I'm his daughter! Mark, Brad, and I were sitting in front of two screens and Will Ferrell and the other guy were in the boat—a yellow raft. Right down the road was a park and that's where they shot some exteriors. Now they had built the exterior in the interior and there were men walking around in rubber up to their breasts because there was water everywhere. Will and Anna were in the raft and there were guys all around the raft like waiters. Then there was the character, Will, sitting on the boat up front because he was gonna direct this ride—it's a ride! The Rick Marshall character said, "Is this part of the ride?" and the Will character responded, "There are no show tunes on this boat." Then there's a small earthquake, like an aftershock. Ferrell's got all this equipment strapped on him and it falls off into the water and he keeps saying, "Shit! Oh shit!" I was in hysterics from laughter because when I did the show, I wasn't even allowed to say, "Oh my God!" They'd yell, "Cut!" and remind me I had to say, "Oh, my gosh!" Here he was saying "shit" and that was a scream. Spencer said it off-screen back in the day, but here, after 35 years, they actually brought the word "shit" into the dialogue.

Oh, and remember how I said that Brad, the director, had told us to just park there where we had met him? Well, about 20 minutes into the filming, a man approached us asking if that was our white Cadillac parked outside. Prior to us reaching the soundstage, Mark had been "Mario-ing" it (as in racing legend Mario Andretti), driving his white Cadillac like a nutcase through the back lot. I thought the guy was going to ticket us. Instead, he informed us that we were blocking the famous Universal tour tram from its hourly route.

Everyone was very nice, though, and made us feel warm

193

and welcome. After an hour or so on stage 27, Brad asked if we wanted to check out the other stages. 29 was absolutely incredible. Now this is what I'm talking about! Moss, vines, webs, and vegetation of all types hung from the 30-foot plus ceilings. Very exotic! You could actually see where some of that $200 million budget was spent on that stage. It was so freaky because amongst all the greenery were some Sleestak heads that were about 30 feet tall! They were so dramatic looking that it tripped that magical feeling inside me, very similar to the first time I saw the scene in *Jurassic Park* where the brontosaurus crosses the prairie. That particular scene made me feel like these creatures were mine, like I had a connection to them that others in the audience did not own. Tears poured down my cheeks and fell into my jaw-dropping mouth. Mark kept saying over and over, "Wow, this is really cool," but it's one thing for someone who wasn't a part of this to look at it and another for someone that grew up on it. I just broke into tears, because it's a part of my life. *Land of the Lost* just won't let me go. Not too many people can say they rode a baby brontosaurus.

We saw Marty Krofft while we were there, too. I pointed him out to Mark and we went over to him. He said, "I remember you,"—and he held his hand out to indicate four feet tall—"when you were that little." You know who is really lovely? His brother, Sid. He called me up early one morning during that period and it was just the cutest conversation. He was the last person I would expect to call me on a Saturday morning. He said he had a hard time getting my phone number. He said some lighting guy had it so he got it from him. Sounded crazy to me. No idea who that could have been. Sid had been just sitting there with my phone number, though, because he didn't want to call me too early. Now, mind you, he's like in his 80s or something. The sound in his voice was so sweet, like an older person. Like I said before, he's the creative genius behind everything of the world of Sid and Marty Krofft. I told him, "You know what? I am so proud to be part of the family of Sid and Marty Krofft."

There had been talk of Wesley and me doing a cameo for the film. A few weeks into the shooting, I received a phone call from the Wardrobe Department asking me for a convenient time to have a fitting. Whoa! That had to be a good sign! A week later they were at my house with their tape measure out. My numbers were weird but easy to remember: 30-30-30, the same measurements I'd had back in the day. I think they call that a 12-year-old boy. Anyway, it wasn't too long after the fitting that I received a package at my apartment from FedEx with "sides" (a portion of a script) in it. My name was stamped on the cover page in big print—KATHLEEN COLEMAN—and the rest of the pages, about eight in total, were highlighted under the name, "Holly." Well let's see. They were sent to my door, with my name on the front and I had been Holly so don't you think I just assumed they were mine? It made perfect sense. I was so excited! I remember studying them but having a hard time memorizing them because they didn't sound like anything I would say, even as an adult. So now I had an outfit on the way and a few lines to spit out. When do I get to be a movie star? It's funny. Throughout my childhood, people used to think life must be so easy for me, what with being a movie star and all. I always corrected them and told them I wasn't a movie star. I had only done theater and television. But finally here I was, about to be a real movie star!

When we arrived, the set was absolutely phenomenal. We actually were able to film our scene at the La Brea Tar Pits. You look at these dinosaurs and you just can't even imagine that they were actually standing right there. That's just so neat. You could trip out about that forever! They were actually IN this particular property! We were standing on the ground and there was oil coming up from the grass. Then there are huge mammoths and saber-toothed tigers and all the gigantic dinosaurs inside the museum. So nutty! It was all just a gas and a half!

Kathy Coleman

So we arrived on set and I was telling everybody I was ready to go. I had my lines memorized. Brad, the director, said, "What lines?" He said, "That's the funniest thing I've heard in a long time. You don't have any lines!" They had sent me "Holly's" lines but it wasn't me. Here I go and memorize it all and it wasn't for me at all. Why they sent those script pages to me nobody knew. We're still puzzled about that even now. Everyone thought it was all a big funny ha-ha, but I didn't think it was funny at all. I told the director he'd better come up with a line for me or I was going to make one up for myself, even if I had to fall over a cord or something and yell, "Ouch!" Something!

The very reason that I wanted to do this whole project is that it had such a major effect on so many other people's lives. My kids were running around, my friends, my boyfriend was all excited, my sister called me from work. The one thing it should be, above all, is fun. El bingo! That's all I wanted. And it basically was a fun shoot. There was a lot of pressure and stress, though. If you work on a movie the whole time, you adjust yourself to the odd hours; but I didn't, so I hadn't adjusted. It was just, like, bam! Makeup and wardrobe. They put me in a not-so-great wardrobe, but they did great hair and makeup. I looked like half a million bucks! That was so much fun. In my trailer dressing room, they had my wardrobe on the hangers, all lined up, and there were lots of bras and, maybe five girdles.

One of the girdles, though, was the most jumbo girdle I'd ever seen! "I've got to wear a girdle?" I asked.

And the wardrobe lady says, "Well, you don't have to, but we kinda recommend it."

Now, I'm so tiny but I do have a poochy belly just because I've had children. Actually I've always had that. Been with me since I was a little girl. But a girdle? Whatever!

I said, "Oh, strap me in, I don't care." There was a black one that had I put it on it would've gone up over my boobs. I said, "What do you want me to do with this one?" I pulled it out and it was about four feet long. I was supposed to put that thing on and a bra! I could've gone surfing in that! It was like a wetsuit. I would've been attacked by a great white in that girdle. But I eventually wound up with just a little girdle on. I wore it.

They did set interviews with me and still photography and I had on big sunglasses, super-huge, like Bozo the Clown sunglasses, but they were shaped like stars. And I said, "You know what, I've never done film before. I've done theater and television but today, I am a movie star ... so get out of my way, road hog!" I just was having so much fun with it. When I was in makeup they dared me to go onto the set with the sunglasses on. So I did. "No autographs, please. No autographs."

It was really a very cool experience up to a point. I sat with Will Ferrell for a while. I just walked up to him; he was just sitting there and I said, "Can I sit with you?" We just talked about how the whole show had come to fruition. I had been told that he was the one who got it all going. He said, "I would love to tell you that it was me but it really wasn't. It was Universal. And I kinda got pulled in at the end." He was very different from what you'd expect. Very soft spoken. You're not going to get SNL out of him. Nice, well-spoken, and very polite, but not what you would think.

I got to meet the writer who seemed cool at the time, just a really neat guy. I didn't realize yet just how bad this thing was going to turn out to be. He was talking to me while I was sitting next to Will. We were all just cackling. No one ever claimed a hierarchy. Will Ferrell never said, "Oh, I can't wait to meet you." He couldn't have cared less. It was just, "It's nice to meet you."

I got sick round about 11:30, 12, something like that. Must have been the chicken. They put on, I would guesstimate, a crew of about 2000 and I would say probably a $20,000 dollar meal that they served from 7-9. Unreal! Five catering trucks! One was Chinese, one was steaks, one was chicken, and one was only salads. It was just unbelievable.

I was on the set and I suddenly thought about that place in the back of my throat and next thing you know I was puking in trash buckets everywhere. And I couldn't explain it. I mean how long of a story is that? I used to be bulimic as a child and … how do you describe that? I just blurted out, "Trashcan! Quick, please!" But once I start doing that, I get the chills and I have to have lots of blankets on me. I know it sounds so gross and I'm so sorry to tell you this but it's the truth.

The doctor who was working on me kept saying. "Your vitals are fine." I knew my vitals would be fine. It's all psychological. I get that! I'm just thinking of stuff. I'm not sick. She said, "It is so perfectly normal for you to have this experience. First of all you're not accustomed to being up this late and working 'til all hours of the morning and it's freezing cold. So obviously you're going to have the chills. And you keep going from a set that is so hot, back to your trailer, which is freezing. Doesn't surprise us. But all your vitals—blood pressure, pulse, temp, everything else—all normal."

But I could not stop puking! I went into the doctor's trailer and just curled up with a bunch of blankets because I was shivering so badly. I kept asking the doctor if they needed me back on the set. There's no way, after 35 years, I didn't care how damn sick I was, that I wasn't going to get this done! They would keep me abreast, she told me. They want me now? No, no, no. They're still working on another scene. Oh, goody. Pulled the covers back over me. Mind you, I had already been through all that makeup, hair and wardrobe, you'll remember, and I didn't want to mess anything up. So I'm sleeping like a stiff. It's hard to be sick and not mess up my makeup.

They finally sent word they were ready for me on the set.

"Do you think you can do this? If we don't think you can, we can't allow you back on the set."

I said, "Oh, god no! I'm gonna somehow pull from wherever I have the energy. I cannot mess this up."

Run, Holly, Run!

So I said I was good to go. Shivering. They got me a warm Alaskan coat. They walked me on the set and all of a sudden I started feeling even wonkier. I'm standing up there and it was just a back shot and I said, "You know what? I really cannot do this."

So I went and sat down in these little box chairs right there in the museum. They've got the whole scene up and lit and ready and I'm just sitting on the box feeling like I'm about to flat-out collapse. Anna came over and I told her I really could not do it.

She squatted down on the floor next to me and said, "No. You can!"

I told her I felt like something bad was going to happen.

She said, "No, it isn't. I promise you."

People kept asking, "Why did you get sick? You're ruining it for everybody." But I didn't do it on purpose! I just got sick. Get over it. Wesley got mad at me. Had it not been for Anna's energy, being so positive, I would not have gotten through that last scene. But I did.

For the scene, Ferrell's Rick Marshall walks by us and Wesley, my TV brother, hands him a parking ticket. Because he's a frustrated scientist and he's been looking for validation all his life, Wesley asks, "Can I validate you?" and Ferrell says "No thanks. I've been validated." This is the humor of the film. When he does that, he walks by me and I turn around to the camera and say, "Now that was just rude!" And that's the end of the movie. I got the last line in the picture!

Before we shot, Wesley asked, "What is my line?"

I was so embarrassed. I only had one line and I couldn't remember it either. "Something about validating that ticket you have in your hand," I answered him.

He said, "That's right. 'Do you need to be validated?'" It was just the freakiest thing and I'd have been so humiliated about my own line if not for the fact that he had asked me just about 20 minutes before what *his* line was. I knew mine was something like "That was rude." We were doing all different angles of the shot so it was important to do the exact same line.

And I said, "Did I say, 'That was JUST so rude?' or 'That was rude?' Did I put a 'just' in there?"

Wesley said, "Beats me." Jeez. Thanks a lot! Now I'm gonna have to ask somebody else and make myself look like an idiot that I can't remember one single line.

Once that shot was done, I went back to the medical trailer, crawled into bed and pulled the covers over me. But then the set closed down and, I'm not kidding you, in about a half hour, all that equipment from the set was in the trucks. You can't believe how much stuff was on that set and how fast they were able to all work like marching ants and get it all packed up in those trucks and off they went. And I was just sitting there watching them in my Alaskan coat freezing to death. I was done. I saw Anna Friel walk by me and she gave me a thumbs up. She's the one who had actually pulled me out of my stupor. She was just so magnetic. So much energy that she was able to get me to finish my part. I thought, God bless you, you know?

The wardrobe people had told me all the clothing had to be accounted for because they'd rented it and they'd be in trouble. My friend brought his car around and I told them I couldn't take off the clothing right then because I was just too cold. So here's the jacket and here's the boots, but don't ask me to take off any more clothing because I'm sick and I'm freezing. So I left my green velvet jacket and leather boots. Those were the two most expensive items but the sweater, the bra, the girdle, the pants and the stockings came home with me.

I called Wesley the next day because he was really concerned and I said, "I just wanna let you know I'm feeling better. I'm all right. Hydrated myself and I feel better."

He said, "I'm gonna tell you. I'm hurt and I'm pissed. I missed my close-up!"

I was thinking, close-up of what? The back of your head? I couldn't believe he was actually angry at that.

He said, "Do you know how many years I've been waiting for this?"

Excuse me? Same amount I'd been! No difference there. Why would I deliberately wreck this when my life was on the line as well? I just happened to get sick. If it had happened to you, I'd have been right there in your corner. I went down for a little while, but they didn't need me then so who cares if I'm sitting in my trailer or lying in a hospital room at that time? It didn't really matter. This isn't the be all and end all of my life.

So, yeah, it was kind of crazy and of course Wesley and I got over our irritation with the situation and each other, but overall it was a lot of fun being back in that cool world again and having people come up and fool with my hair and say we need to do this and that for you, you know? I hadn't had that in a long time. That used to be my life all the time and I do miss it. Not that I really need it but it was just something that I grew up on—people pulling at my hair so that I looked proper all the time. It was just kind of weird to be back, even briefly.

Once the filming was over, I stayed excited. I figured that most likely after December—certainly no later than early January or February—they'd start promoting *Land of the Lost*. There was a music box. When you opened it, the theme song of *Land of the Lost* played. Cool promotional stuff like that. They also had the coolest T-shirt with the original logo and rocks, only updated. I really wanted them to send me one of those. Sid told me to get myself prepared because a lot of stuff was going to be going on and it was all about to start!

I knew there would be all these trailers coming out and my kids could say, "Look. It's Mama! There she is." All this work I'd been doing all these years, they were finally going to know! THAT'S ME! THERE I AM! I was so excited knowing my kids were going to be able to say, "That's my mother! See!"

After all that work and all that hope and all that excitement, the cameo scene that Wesley and I shot ended up on the cutting room floor. They went with a completely different gag ending. The very worst part of all, though, was that the *Land of the Lost* movie itself ended up being one big, mostly unfunny joke that insulted and disappointed the eagerly awaiting fans of our classic series! I'm over it by this point. Life's too short. Moving on.

Oh, before I forget, I was also in one other movie. In a way. It's called *The Bubble Boy*. It's from 2001 and stars Jake Gyllenhaal. It's actually a funny movie so it's not a total waste of your time but if you watch closely, there's about a 60 second clip of me from the original *Land of the Lost*. You actually see me go riding by on Dopey. Of course as per usual, money and I just don't seem to play well together. Same thing here. I never got anything from that, but it was cool.

CHAPTER 28

The Role of an Actor

I find this profession to be the glue in life. When you tell
people that you are an actor, a lot of times you'll receive
a bit of a sigh as if this is a second-rate line of work. My belief
is that without actors in our society we'd all be in the closet regarding all kinds of issues. Actors share intimate details and
aspects of themselves on the screen. We go to the movies for a
reason. We are able to see with our own eyes and hear with our
own ears that other people do what we always thought was
unique and sometimes even weird about ourselves. It brings a
sense of comfort to know we are not alone in our thoughts and
actions.

I studied with a number of acting coaches. With all the lessons I learned, one stands out. To this day it's the most profound
statement regarding acting I've ever heard. My acting teacher
told me that if I wanted to be a good actor, I had to be able to
stand naked and turn slowly. "Let everyone see every inch of
you. This includes all the usual parts of your body that you
would normally hide."

The comment goes far deeper than just your outer appearance. You need to be able to show your most vulnerable self.
This is what people want to see: that's the glue. It connects us.
Most actors have lived pretty full lives, so they have quite a bit
to draw on. Being an emotional person usually is what drives
them into this industry. I don't think there is an inch of Meryl

Streep's body that she hasn't shared with all of us. She is someone who turns extremely slowly.

I recently worked on a film and had a chance to see some of the dailies (scenes that were shot the day before). In most cases actors are allowed to view these dailies freely. On this particular film my director wouldn't allow me to see mine. Two weeks after the shoot I was called in to do voiceover or looping work. In two of the scenes I was in, my lines were muffled and I needed to redo them. I happened to walk into the studio and see that the director and the sound engineer were watching the first scene I was in. I looked so hideous. The camera must have been a half inch from my face because you could see every flaw... and then some. I'm not kidding, it was painful. Lo and behold those words of wisdom rang in my ears. In that particular scene I was turning so slowly that the camera must have gotten stuck and zoomed in for the shot from hell. What transpired from viewing this was mind-blowing.

A week or so after this appointment, I was called in again. They had added a scene to the end of the film and needed me. I was free, finally able to stand naked (metaphorically of course). There was no way I was ever going to look any worse than what I had already seen. What this provided for me was the freedom to not hide. I could show the most vulnerable sides of myself. As actors we tend to get stuck, too much in our own heads. This feeling I had was so freeing. I was able to get out of my own way. I was so proud of myself. I was never so beautiful.

The scene turned out fantastic by the way. At this time I'm not sure of a release date or if it will be for the big screen or the small one. For me, it's the best work I've ever done, for many reasons.

PART VII
THAT'S A WRAP

CHAPTER 29

Realizations

*Y*ou are a smart person. I'm sure you picked up on the major issues I've dealt with in my life, most of which stemmed from having and not having money. There are plenty of spider legs off that theme: power, control, stress, self-esteem, self-worth, body issues, and on and on. But I'm not ending my story looking for a pity party. Oh no. I'm much better having gone through these things. Like all of us, if we hadn't gone through the challenges of our past, we probably wouldn't be who we are today. So while it sure as hell hasn't been easy, I am grateful for what I have now, and frankly I wouldn't have it without having gone through the crazy and then coming out on the other side.

Over the years I have had to do quite a bit of forgiving. I always go to the "big picture" which is love. I have made so many mistakes and poor decisions throughout my life. I would hate to think love wasn't available for me. I have chosen to remove certain people from my life or at least limit the amount of energy or time I spend in their presence, but not without first putting myself in their shoes. My heart alerts my mind that we are all here to learn our own personal lessons. This is when I feel in my core being that I must love and have compassion for others, so forgiveness is mandatory for me. I may not forget wrong-doings, but I can see what brings people to behave in certain ways, even though I'd like to think those behaviors wouldn't be mine. You just never know.

Love produces many different physical and emotional feelings in me. My two boys, for instance, can produce a lump in
my throat if I think about what they mean to me and the incredibly
close bond we share. When I think about Colleen, a horn of
plenty hits me. I don't know life without her. So a whole slew of
emotions erupt. Peke-A-Boo Jones, now when I think about him,
pure joy fills me. Having him in my life made me feel special.

As for my love life, Mark brings a sigh of relief to me. He's
neither a liar nor a cheat and up until this point my choices in
men have been one of the two ... or both. It's so nice to be free
of that fear and anxiety. The incident in which Mark had me arrested haunted me for a while. No matter how hard I tried, I
couldn't help finding a piece of anger to attach to him. Now in
retrospect, it was probably my biggest wakeup call. So, more
forgiveness for him and myself.

Of course I'm well aware that all of these lessons are or-
chestrated by the universe in which God created. That's very
comforting for me. My belief is that the best way to thank God
is to love yourself. And after all, I chose to be me and all that
goes with it. I don't want, however, to kid myself or you, the
reader. Loving myself at times can be quite a challenge. As long
as I stay out of the past, though, and focus on now, I find it an
easier journey.

Another thing I learned over the years is that anytime I allow
someone to take me out of my rhythm, it's a mistake. I have to
stay true to myself and that was a lesson that was difficult to
learn and even harder to put into practice. The stress that resulted
from that would manifest in very physical ways, from my eating
binges and stomach sicknesses to bedwetting. And something I
haven't told you about yet. I was a nail biter. It's no wonder,
since my stress levels were off the charts. I used to pray that my
agent wouldn't call with an audition for a Mattel toy commercial.
This company was so strict regarding the shape of your hands

and nails if you were in their ads. You were, after all, holding their toys and most shots were close-ups.

Back then, I bit my nails to the quick. After one of those godforsaken calls would come in from my agent, I'd get sick to my stomach. Mum would say to me "let me see what shape your nails are in." I'd show her my hands turned upside-down. She would flip them over, bang the top of my hand with the file and let out a disgusted sigh. She would then begin to file them, cursing the whole time. This procedure was so excruciating that my nails would start bleeding. Once the bleeding stopped she'd apply clear polish and off we'd go to the interview. We both knew I wasn't going to land the job, but we would go anyway. The same quiet ride home and the underlying disappointment permeated the car; it was stifling.

Another thing I used to do that drove Mum crazy was this thing with my nose. I would twitch my nose back and forth, sort of like a distorted version of *Bewitched*. What followed the twitch of the nose was the smacking of my lips together. Mum would mimic me. Sometimes she would throw a handheld mirror in front of my face and say "Look at what you're doing!" I had no idea. My nose just bothered me and whatever it took to make it stop was what I did.

As I've gotten older, all of those issues I had back then no longer exist. I even wear bangs now. Back when I was a teenager I seemed to be the only one with bangs and I hated them. You couldn't feather bangs. They were too short for that. Mum would never let me grow them out. Like I said, the things you go through are what make you who you are today. So I hope you understand that I may bitch and moan about Mum, but I truly loved her. She did the very best she could and I wouldn't have had my successes without her. I miss her dearly. We'd have been fun together today.

Speaking of today, recently a good friend of mine took her own life. I bring this up because I believe there are two types of people in the world. I'm pretty sure I could go toe to toe on the subjects of my eventful childhood and my rock 'em sock 'em adulthood with anyone. I've never been interested in sympathy. In fact, it embarrasses me. What does interest me is the strength you achieve, the drive to push forward. I don't discount people's depression. I've been plenty depressed before, myself. I chose to take "alone downtime" to get to know myself. I've had quite a few intimate conversations with me. What I've noticed is exactly what the saying "time heals everything" means.

Not every issue magically disappears, but they can each be viewed from a less severe angle. For instance, I've gone to bed with a head loaded with sadness and woken up to moments of clarity. I was still sad, but had hope. When my kids were young I used to use the f-word a lot. Only the f-word in our house was "function." Whenever there were moments of sadness or any of the other negative feelings, I would always drop the f-bomb. You'd be amazed just how fast those emotions leave when you start to function. Especially if you do something for someone else.

But back to money and its power over me. Someone once said to me, "It doesn't take much to make you happy." The thing is that this wasn't the first person who had said something like that to me. When I first heard this I felt like someone had tacked a sign on my forehead that read, "I think poor thoughts." This bothered me. I've been around plenty of money and seen many fancy things. Why did they see *that* in me? Actually for years this bothered me until one day I flipped the switch on it.

I came up with my own version of "poor thoughts." I started saying, "Well, in life things come and go. And when times are tough, guess who's still going to be happy?" I thought this was pretty insightful and it worked for a while. But still the message was delivered to me that I didn't strive for enough.

So who am I today, you might ask. Let's start with my name. Now I know I have had many a name, but something in the last

20 years has been very puzzling to me. Nine out of ten times when people ask me what my name is, this is the crazy thing that occurs:

"What's your name?"

I answer, "Kathleen."

"Do you like to be called something else?"

Me, "No."

"Do you have a nickname?"

Me again, "You mean like 'Ralph'?"

Why bother asking me my name when they only want to change it? I meet people all the time and when they tell me their name I have no desire to change it for them. I take it at face value. You tell me your name is Jeff and that works for me. No need to call you Sam. I bust people on this all the time. For instance, I was in the hospital not too long ago having surgery, for crying out loud. When filling out the paperwork my nurse asked me what my name is. I told her.

She said, "Do you go by anything else?"

"I've been known to use 'Ralph.'" Here's where I thought I'd get back at her on my terms. I came out of surgery, right? Well, she wanted to see if the anesthetic had worn off and I was back on planet earth.

She asked, "Do you know where you are?"

"Yes, I'm in the hospital."

"Do you know your name?"

I answer, "Yes. Cinderella." At first she was quiet, and then I started laughing. It was becoming comical to me. But in reality do you think my mother named her three daughters Maureen, Colleen, and Kathleen for nothing?

One name that I'm called all the time that has never bothered me is "Holly." It would have been hard for Mum to come up with three girl names to rhyme with Holly, but I wouldn't mind having that name. Colleen did name her daughter Holly and I'm very honored by that.

CHAPTER 30

We Are Not Alone

*S*o, yeah. I have had a really rough ride, but it's just the journey I signed up for. *Run, Holly, Run!* is the perfect title for this book because as you can plainly see, I've been running for most of my life. First I was hustling to get work as a little girl. Then when I did get the job, everything had finally paid off, and I was literally running on the TV show, but it was a perfect metaphor for how I felt at that time. My family depended on me to keep going, keep earning an income, and I did.

I didn't realize then that running from Grumpy and the Sleestaks was the easy part. It seemed like an idyllic life for a child. Here I was living in a cave, riding a baby dinosaur, speaking a whole new language with my Pakuni friend and on and on. It was a job, but it was pretty special and magical. Out of that came more than anyone could ever predict: inappropriate behavior on the set, a lost feeling once the show was unceremoniously cancelled, and then the expectation that I could repeat the process and book another show like that.

Inferiority is kind of a weird feeling. I've had fleeting moments of this feeling almost too silly to mention. For instance, Mum used to say that I would never be Farrah Fawcett. My boyfriend Mark pointed to just about every woman on TV and asked me, "Why can't you be more like her?" Maybe he was kidding; but once again, these people think I'm some sort of magician. They don't seem to get the God thing—that he just produces one-of-a-kinds.

Despite all the body image issues I've gone through, I like the place that I've found myself these days. I really do. I like being comfortable in my own skin finally because at times I've been so uncomfortable. I wasn't pretty enough, skinny enough, all of that. That's a hard road for anyone to walk. I'm still going through a little bit of that right now because I have a few weirdie things happening to my body.

I have to wear glasses these days. I was fine for years. I was fine right up until 39 years and 364 days but then, bam! Somebody handed me my birthday card and I couldn't read it. Right on the day. What the hell just happened? So I had to get bifocals. Bifocals make you so freakin' dizzy. Where we used to live, it was 52 steps up to our place from where we parked. Try going downstairs with bifocals. Go ahead. I dare you!

And that darn old gravity. I look at it this way. At least it keeps me connected to the earth. I don't know how your feelings are on this, but to constantly be in that kind of light that you're being looked upon for your success—you go to work and do your job. What if your job required you to be absolutely beautiful every single day? It's really crazy, right? Then after you've done that all these years and things start to change, you have a couple of kids and all of a sudden the bikini doesn't look the same. You start getting wrinkles around your eyes and people say things to you like, "Looking a little old there." I would never say that to anybody. My sister even says it to me all the time. She's heavy. She says no one in a million years would ever come up to her and say, "Boy, are you fat!" But she says, "I watch people do it to you constantly." People do come up to me and say some of the rudest, cruelest things. Did they think that life wasn't going to hit me for some reason? Do they not realize how much time has passed? I find those people to be so clueless. I really do. I see some older celebs and, for me, what I get out of it is, "Boy, you did the time." It's kind of how prisoners look at each other. You did your time.

The aging process is lovely, and no one should take that away from you by saying, "Well, you don't look as good as you used to." I don't think I want to look 12 anymore. I know I'm not what I was even at 25 or 35 or whatever, but you know what? I like what's inside of me. That's what I like and you can kiss my ever-lovin' rear end … which, as I mentioned earlier, is really not looking too good these days. I really am a pretty well-adjusted human being for having been in show business. There are a lot of people who have been through this business and have been raked over the coals. You know what? Show business didn't do that to me. I wouldn't allow it. Oh, it had me in its grip for a little while, but thank God I was able to pull out of it.

I'm very aware of my surroundings at all times because of all my martial arts training. Starting from the age of 10, I studied four different styles, including Okinawa-Te and Jiu Jitsu. When you get attacked, part of the rush for attackers is the element of surprise. You will never catch me that way. I have panoramic views of my world. We all have our own rhythm, our own dance. If you really think about it, people constantly try to take you out of your rhythm by saying or doing something that makes you almost trip over your own feet. Don't ever let anybody take you out of your rhythm.

All of us as individuals are on our own journey. In times of crisis, people may throw their arms around you to comfort you. Not that this doesn't help or isn't appreciated; it's just that the pain you're feeling is barricaded inside of you where no one else can get to. So you're alone in this moment. I know you've heard the saying, you come into this world alone and you leave alone. So yes, we are all alone, but the common bond *is* that we are all alone. In that sense we are all alone together. This is why I believe the role of an actor is so valuable. It emphasizes just how similar we all are. And for brief moments, you and that

character can be on the same page, wavelength, mindset, or whatever way you personally experience the feeling that other people share some of the same goofy thoughts and feelings as you.

~

I have been blessed with so many wonderful gifts in my life, with Chris and Phonzo, of course, being my favorites. They are just so crazy terrific. My sister Colleen, without whom life just wouldn't be the same. She's my anchor. Mark: he's my secret strength and I'm keeping him all for myself. I love my friends that I've had for forever and also the newer ones who've joined on. Thanks to Herbie J Pilato. And let's not forget my angel of angels, Peke-A-Boo Jones.

And I guess that's about it. Like I stated in the beginning of the book, I hope you feel like we sat down and had a conversation: some laughs, some tears, and a good heaping handful of, "Oh, my God! *THAT happened?*" My journey is far from over. I know I've learned many lessons along the way and yet have many more to come. I welcome them. Through all the swings and punches, giggles and tears, I'm still smiling that lemon smile I was born with and plan to carry for many moons and sunrises ahead.

From the bottom of my happy heart, my friend, I thank you for our conversation.

EPILOGUE

Searching for Spencer

*F*or the past few years, Wesley, Phil, and I have been attending the comic-con conventions. During these events they have
what are called panels; this is where the celebrities from a particular show sit up on a stage in one of the hotel's mini-ballrooms.
Many attendees come to the panels to listen to the stories we tell
and they are allowed to ask questions of each of us. Usually
these questions pertain to what is happening in our lives now
and if there is any news regarding the show (*Land of the Lost*).
Well, a few years back we filmed a documentary. We have been
promising the release of this at every panel since then. Talk
about a clusterfuck. This documentary is a non-scripted journey
the three of us went on in the state of Wisconsin. We were in this
particular state because that is where Spencer lives. With the exception of my visit with him on my 18th birthday, none of us had
seen him since the close of the second season of the show, some
forty years ago.

In order to tell this story and have it make any sense, I need
to give you some prior details that led up to this adventure. It all
began with a fan of mine on Facebook. I'm just going to refer to
him as Tom. Tom lived in Wisconsin and owned a memorabilia
museum and was a huge fan of the show. He and I worked out a
deal for me to do a personal appearance and sign autographs at
his establishment. He, of course, took care of airfare, hotel, and
the normal fee I charge for appearances.

Run, Holly, Run!

My boyfriend Mark grew up in Wisconsin and because I had never been to his hometown, he decided to join me on this excursion. The plan was for me to do the meet and greet, and then afterwards I'd hang out with Mark. Before I left Los Angeles, Tom and I had many a conversation regarding what I could expect upon my arrival. Some of these details included a guest list of about 400 attendees who were expected to show up at his museum. On the scheduled day, I arrived with felt marker in hand, and to my surprise about 15 people were there, all with big smiles and some even wearing those Sleestak costumes you can purchase online. Those 15 folks turned out to be Tom's relatives. The other 385 people were non-existent.

At first this made me a little nervous. Tom, however, assured me that he was perfectly happy for me to just hang out with his family and all my fees would still be paid. Oh, well. Turns out these people were fabulous. After spending the day with them, I felt like one of the family. Tom and I bonded right away; super nice guy and had a terrific business, and family to boot. I signed many pictures and took a slew of photos with the gang. When this was all said and done, Tom drove me back to my hotel where I was to then meet up with Mark. Because these parts are his old stomping grounds, Mark was eager to play tour guide.

Over the course of the day, Spencer's name came up and even the town that he lived in. Mark knew of this town and offered to go on a wild goose chase in search of him. I can't even begin to explain all the synchronistic events that took place, down to the log cabin we were directed to, that all brought us to within one mile of Spencer's front doorstep. It was the lady at the check-in desk who overheard Mark and me talking about Spencer and then proceeded to tell us that he lived a mile down the road. Unbelievable!

Before we made a mad dash down to his house, I suggested to Mark that we invite my new friend Tom to join us. I said to Mark, "Meeting Spencer would blow this guy away. Let's give him that gift." So we waited the three and a half hours for Tom to drive to us before we ventured off to Spencer's. Needless to say, Tom was beside himself with joy. The three of us were in Mark's car—a black Cadillac—and we headed down the long driveway and lo and behold there was Spencer, getting out of his car. He must have just arrived there minutes before us.

He looked at our car with a not-so-happy expression on his face. The two guys stayed in the car while I got out. Spencer took one look at me and instantly his face changed from a scowl to the loving man I remembered. We spent the whole afternoon with him at the house and went to dinner with him and his wife later that evening. During the afternoon visit, Spencer asked me to follow him into his big old barn. We spoke of many subjects, from me having children to him mowing the lawn on his riding mower. The funniest coincidence came about in the conversation. I don't know exactly how we got on this subject, but it turned out one of his favorite books is *Mutant Message* as well. I was pleasantly surprised, but not shocked.

After a very nice dinner, Spencer asked Mark and me what time we get up in the morning. We told him early. In a very matter-of-fact tone, he told us he'd be at our cabin at 7:00 a.m. As promised, he showed up right at 7:00 the next morning and he had a much different attitude than he'd had the day before. First, he and Mark talked about business regarding future *LOTL* proposals. Tom had many ideas that he'd tossed out to us the day before. Tom was a very successful businessman and had some interesting plans for the four original cast members. They ranged from marketing ideas to possible shows throughout the Midwest. I think it was the topic of marketing that set Spencer off. The venting energy I picked up on earlier from Spencer was about to burst. And boy did it ever.

He got on a roll about Marty Kroft and the flood gates opened. I could see beads of sweat forming on Spencer's brow and I almost thought I saw steam coming out of his ears. He was furious that none of us saw one nickel from the merchandise they sold of the show. That, in fact, is why he left. He had tried to get a share for all of us and they wouldn't budge. Do you realize how many lunchboxes were sold?

It's always been weird to me to see my face all over coloring books, chapter books, game boards, t-shirts, and of course the lunchboxes and know that we didn't get one shiny dime from any of it. So anyway, I continued to observe Mark and Spencer's conversation. I couldn't help but think how proud I was of Spencer and my connection to him. Not only were we on the same show together, but for all intents and purposes he was my dad. And that's exactly how I felt. The whole weekend had been fabulous. I felt very proud of myself. I was able to do something that not even Universal Studios could do, which was to find Spencer Milligan. Well, this visit started the wheels a-spinnin'!

Between Mark, Tom, and I, we had come up with an idea to make a documentary. It would be a gift to the fans after the *LOTL* movie had not only disappointed, but had also put some to sleep. Tom offered to finance this project. This would include airfare, hotels, camera crew, and a van to transport all of us from Milwaukee to Spencer's town. The premise of this documentary was to film the original cast, non-scripted, all along a three-hour drive. The plan was to have each of us tell stories of our favorite memories with Spencer and each other. We'd also talk about some behind-the-scenes moments that had never before been shared.

My job in all of this was to gather up Wesley and Phil, not an easy task. I had to juggle around everyone's schedules to get us all on separate planes arriving at about the same time. Another duty I took on was to alert the media of our plan and coordinate the announcement of our arrival in Spencer's town. So I called the news stations, the local radio shows, and a few local newspapers. Everyone was not only surprised, but very excited that we would be bringing this event to their town. The restaurant that Mark and I had dined in on our previous trip offered to sponsor us. They would put tables out in front so that we could sign autographs. They also would provide us with food and beverages. The people of the town were invited for a meet and greet. All of this was moving along just fine. Planes were booked, hotels arranged, etc.

Over the course of the month-long planning, I had placed hundreds of phone calls, emails, text messages, everything except a homing pigeon. For the life of me I couldn't reach Spencer. It was as if he had disappeared from the face of the earth. My stress level skyrocketed. There was no turning back, too many things were already in motion. I couldn't even bring myself to let the others know that I hadn't gotten Spencer's approval yet. My bad. I was panicking. The day arrived and we were all loaded up in the van, camera guys included.

When we had been on the road about twenty minutes, I let the cat out of the bag. I told everyone that I had not been able to reach Spencer. In my defense and in my mind, I thought, gosh if you all were to do something like this for me I would be so grateful. I would love it if out of the blue, after forty years, my fellow cast mates showed up at my door. We had instructed our two camera guys not to film Spencer without his permission. Filming us in the van on that three-hour drive was free game. And really if that's all there was to offer the fans, it would have been great in itself. We had named the documentary *Searching for Spencer*, so the searching part didn't exactly mean finding him.

We showed up in the town in the early afternoon. As promised, the restaurant had set out tables and umbrellas. They had also hung posters of us in their windows. I continued to call Spencer to no avail. I would say about 100 people showed up. They brought items for us to sign, and we had also brought photos to hand out. The media even came by and we did an interview with them. Keep in mind all of this was being filmed by our crew as well. It was good stuff. As the crowd thinned out, we decided to wrap it up and make a last ditch effort to see Spencer. I knew where he lived, so off we went. Very nervous, all of us. What would his reaction be if he was home? Hopefully good, but we were still scared. Well, you can only imagine how my stomach was in knots. Although this endeavor would inevitably be my responsibility, everyone in the van had played a part in the fiasco.

We arrived at his long driveway, which only intensified the nerves of all of us. Wesley, Phil, and I had planned to go up to the door by ourselves and leave everyone else in the van. This included Mark, Tom, the camera guys, the driver, and a friend of Tom's. It was a big van. And before leaving Milwaukee, Mark and I had gone to an office supply store and purchased big black, block sticker letters. We spelled out *Land of the Lost* on either side of the white van. We were not coming into Spencer's town unnoticed. Heaven help us. To the door the three of us went. Knock, knock. The front door opened, but the screen was left shut so the person on the other side was blurry. There was nothing blurry about the voice behind the door though. It was Spencer's wife. This sweet lady who I'd met on my first visit was sweet no more. She in no uncertain terms told me to get the fuck off her property. She said that I had betrayed them and their trust.

I stood there with my mouth dropped open because I couldn't believe my ears. This was a dagger straight to my heart. My intention was never to do one ounce of harm. She didn't even know the camera guys were there at this point. I collected myself as quickly as possible and asked if she would at least allow Wesley and Phil to see Spencer. I would leave the property while they visited. She responded with this comment: "I don't even know if Spencer wants to see them." I just stood my ground and didn't say anything. As I was trying to remove the dagger from my heart, it got shoved in again. Only this time not by her, but Wesley and Phil. One of them said, "We should be able to see him because we didn't have anything to do with the betrayal." Totally threw me under the bus. I turned and walked away. My feelings were so hurt and I had to go back to the van with all of these emotions swirling around inside me.

Of course, everyone in the van wanted to know what had happened. I told the driver to back the van off the property now! We drove for about a mile or so before he pulled over on the side of the road. The firestorm of questions started up from everyone. After what I'd experienced, my explanation came out very weepy and childlike. I knew what I had done was still wrong, despite my intentions. I should have talked to Spencer first. I just got so caught up in the excitement of it all that I had lost my judgement.

As you probably know, when you mix hurt, guilt, and sadness together, anger usually follows. Boy, did it ever. I let loose like a wild banshee. All the pent-up anxiety of this whole trip came flying out of me. What I didn't realize when I finally stopped my rampage was that the two camera guys had been filming the entire time. I was devastated. Strangely enough, the guys in the van almost simultaneously agreed that this footage would be the best part of the documentary!

I felt like a truck had just run over me and they were thinking it was great stuff. Now here's how the whole thing unfolded on Spencer's side. I found out that one afternoon prior to our arrival, he had ventured into town to do some banking. The teller, who he'd probably known forever, mentioned that she'd seen the newspaper about the whole cast coming to town with a camera crew and everything. Well, I'm sure this made Spencer's mouth drop open as wide as mine did when I was told to exit his property stage left. He apparently didn't like surprises any more than I do.

During my first visit with Spencer and his wife, they had mentioned a watering hole that he could be found at just about any night of the week. This was where all his Irish drinking buddies would hang out. They also made it clear that this was past tense; he no longer went there. Once again, lo and behold guess where we ended up driving to? Spencer's bar. Everybody in the joint knew him and had missed his company. I think we had been there about an hour when my phone rang. It was Wesley telling me that Spencer wanted me to come back. Now that was a shocker. So we all piled back into the van and headed back up the road again.

With my tail between my legs and feeling like a recycled rescue dog, I once again asked everyone in the van to stay put. There was no way in hell I was opening that can of worms. Can you imagine returning with lights, camera, action behind me? I walked up to the front porch and I saw Wesley, Phil, and Spencer sitting on deck chairs. Everyone was smiling and sending forgiving energy my way. Spencer stood up and came toward me with his arms open and hugged me. He whispered, "I would have liked to have known."

And that was that. We all sat around on the porch laughing and talking. A few of the topics that we shared were pretty cool, one being a painting that had been brought to us at the restaurant earlier in the day. The woman who gave it to us said that Spencer's father had painted it. Well, sure enough when we showed it to him, he acknowledged that indeed it was his dad's work. He wound up giving it to Phil. The other topic we discussed was the book *Mutant Message*. Wesley had read it, too. At one point, Spencer excused himself and went into the house. When he returned he was holding two hand puppets to communicate with us. One was a rabbit and I think the other was a bear or squirrel. He began using the puppets and at first it was funny, but then it became weird and at times downright strange. I certainly was uncomfortable and from the looks of it, so were the others. I had had enough so I excused myself. I told them I was going to sit with the guys in the van. I hugged Spencer and his puppets and left. I walked away thinking that was self-serving on Spencer's part. Out of character for him. My memory of him was not this. Maybe twenty minutes passed when we saw all of them heading out to the backyard. The whole time I was in the van I had kept quiet. So much had happened in such a short amount of time that my brain needed a break. Before the three of them hit the driveway, they stopped. Words were exchanged and then Wesley and Phil came toward the van. Once again, unbeknownst to me, the camera guys were filming that moment, too. So they did get Spencer on film. They broke the rule we had set for them. DO NOT FILM SPENCER WITHOUT HIS APPROVAL.

The backstory pretty much ends here. Now moving forward, Tom had a prior agreement with the cameraman/director that he would film and edit this project. He was paid in full for both of these duties. He was to take all the footage back to L.A. for editing. He was confident that he could put together a documentary that we would all be happy with. Back in Milwaukee, we said our goodbyes and everyone got on their respective flights. The camera guy had told us that it would probably take somewhere in the neighborhood of two months to complete. Believe me, I needed two months to recoup from this emotional roller-coaster.

Another wave of stress came along when the decision needed to be made about Spencer's cameo role. Do we leave it in or cut it? We were all given a link to view the completed documentary. I thought it turned out very well. Wesley thought I came across too harsh during my van scene. And Phil wasn't crazy about the narration. The real problem was going to be with Spencer viewing it. He would hear all the things I said in the van, and trust me I let loose with some doozies. There is also a part when I talked about the responsibility of being an actor. You sign up for the whole package, not just the parts you like. I think this was described best by a couple I heard talking at a red carpet event. The husband was a successful actor and when he saw all the cameras flashing and all the fans screaming, he rolled his eyes at his wife. She looked at him and said, "Remember, this, *too*, was part of the dream." Very powerful.

I understand privacy but you'd never know it if you heard me screaming and ranting in that van. I'm pretty sure I had a few choice words for his wife thrown in. So I was a little nervous for him to view that scene in particular. I figured, though, it was the truth. I do believe as actors you sign up for giving the fans as much as you can. They are the ones who put you in a place where you even need to make a decision like that. Fame carries a two-sided price tag. Sometimes it works for you and other times you have to work for it.

Well, having said all that, to my and everyone else's surprise, Spencer viewed the documentary and actually liked it! That was a hurdle I never thought we'd get over in a million years. The next hurdle I didn't expect, nor did anyone else. It came from out of the blue. On that three-hour drive from Milwaukee to Spencer's town, we heard over and over from the people in the van what an honor it was for them to be a part of this project. When we were putting all of this together in the beginning we never thought about contracts. So stupid. The loudest voice in the van was Tom's friend. Oh he ranted and raved about how lucky he was to be a witness to all these great stories he was hearing from us.

Turns out he wouldn't sign a release form. His face was in every shot, so just cutting him out was impossible. The plot thickens. Come to find out he was shacking up with the camera guy! He convinced him not to sign a release form either. This infuriated me. The so-called executive producer, Tom, stuck his head in the sand like an ostrich. He was the only one in the position to fight this and he did nothing about it. The documentary was never going to be a money-maker, but these two drew up contracts demanding twenty percent each of any proceeds. This enraged me. The TV show had cut us out of the merchandizing money; that was one thing, and that was pretty bad. But this?

These were our stories, owned by no one but us. How dare anyone who didn't live through this expect to take twenty percent of our lives? Total bullshit.

I thought that my hands were tied and this project would just be shelved. Two years it stayed in the hands of the camera guy (where it remains today). Then he and his live-in buddy tried to show it at comic-con in San Diego. Not on my watch. I drafted up a letter and sent it out to everyone involved, stating that I would sue to the fullest extent of the law anyone who tried to show that documentary. I don't like being held hostage in my own house. This became a matter of principle. So for now I'm saddened and frustrated that this footage may never be seen, and it's a damn shame. The fans would have loved it. My dad, my bad, so sad.

One moment I'll never forget was when Spencer and I were out in front of my cottage hugging one another. I stood back from him and told him right then and there how I had watched all the little girls of the world tell their fathers how proud of them they were, something I never had the opportunity to do. But that day it was finally MY turn. It was so real and so beautiful.

I swear you could see a rainbow right above that fantasy cloud.

EDITOR'S NOTE

Kathleen and Me

BY STEVEN THOMPSON

*O*n November 24th, 1974—Thanksgiving—15 year old me
wrote the following in my daily journal: Happy Thanksgiving! This year, for a change, we stayed home all day. I awoke
early, watched *The Dick Van Dyke Show* and read the paper. I had
pancakes for breakfast and watched the parades. On the whole I
was disappointed with them this year although I did enjoy Kathy
Coleman from *Land of the Lost* singing "Somewhere Over the
Rainbow" as Dorothy.

Life being a series of bizarre coincidences, cut to four
decades later when I discovered that Kathy's lip-synching that
day disguised her tears and confusion caused by the fact that her
mother had just had an epileptic seizure right in front of her on
the way to the parade.

Reality shift.

Here, what had been quite literally a highlight of my holiday
so many years ago now had unknowingly been in the midst of
one of 12-year-old Kathy's biggest nightmares. At the end of the
day, our lives are all about perception. Our perception is our
truth and it's our truth that affects us in life. Truth and facts do
not always coincide.

Being the pop culture buff that I am, a few years ago I was
looking up favorite TV stars of the past to see whatever happened
to some of the ones you never saw anymore. After a while, I
found the notation on the Internet that says Kathy Coleman mar-

ried a millionaire's son and quit show business.

Those two items are facts...but they couldn't be further from the actual truth of her story. For one thing, she isn't even Kathy, she's Kathleen. And Kathleen is the very definition of a survivor.

To see and hear her today is testimony to that fact as her contagious optimism continues to bring her new friends and fans via Facebook and through her appearances at various collector shows and conventions throughout the country.

It was one of those Facebook friends who connected the two of us, in fact, which led to my spending the better part of a year transcribing, retyping, repositioning, laying out and editing her story. Then there were the always delightful telephone calls we shared. If you had told me about all this back when I was 15 and watching the young Kathleen with Wesley Eure and Spencer Milligan on what was surprisingly the most literate sci-fi show on TV, I would never have believed you.

Kathleen's been through several levels of hell in the years since then, but she's still here, and she still loves and cares about life and her fans and the future. As surreal as it all still sometimes seems, I'm proud to call her my friend.

PHOTOS

Photos

Mum about 20 years old

My beautiful mother, 1938

Photos

My famous smile at 10 months old

My first musical, Gypsy, as Baby June (So jazzy!)

Photos

The Shirley Temple look

As Goldilocks in my first commercial, for Shakey's Pizza

Photos

Little Miss La Petite

Photos

A little Marilyn in the house

My prize, Comanche

Photos

Phil and I with our dressing room signs

The Marshall Family

Photos

Phil, my good friend Moosie Drier (*Laugh-In*) and me

My sister Colleen was the President of the *Land of the Lost* Fan Club

Photos

"LAND OF THE LOST"
FAN CLUB

Dear Jane

HI! My name is Colleen. I am the president of the "Land of the Lost"
fan club. I am lucky enough to know the cast of "Land of the Lost" well.

I would like very much for you to become a new member of the club. If
you become a member you will recieve:

Membership Card

8x10 glossy Photo

(Photo shows each cast member separately at the top; at bottom, the
Marshall family is fighting off dinosaur)

Wallet Size Photo

(Photo shows Holly, Rick, Will, and Cha-ka stnading arm in arm in jungle)

Newsletters

(Tells the biographies of Kathy Coleman and Wesley)

Fun Fax

(Tells all the fun little secrets about the whole cast of "Land of the Lost")

Contest

(A contest will be held. The prize winner will recieve an 8x10 autographed
picture by the cast member of your choice)

Memvership kit is $2.00 + 25¢ postage and handling.
If you send a check or money order please make payable to Colleen Buck, not
L. of teh L. fan club, thank-you.

Please write soon!

Sincerely,

Colleen Buck

Colleen Buck
President

Colleen's Fan Club letter

Photos

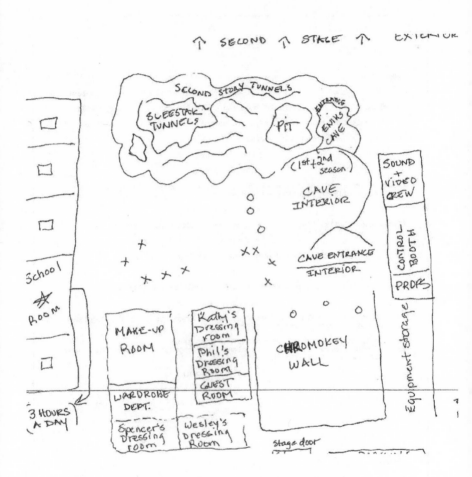

Here are my drawings of the *Land of the Lost* set!

Photos

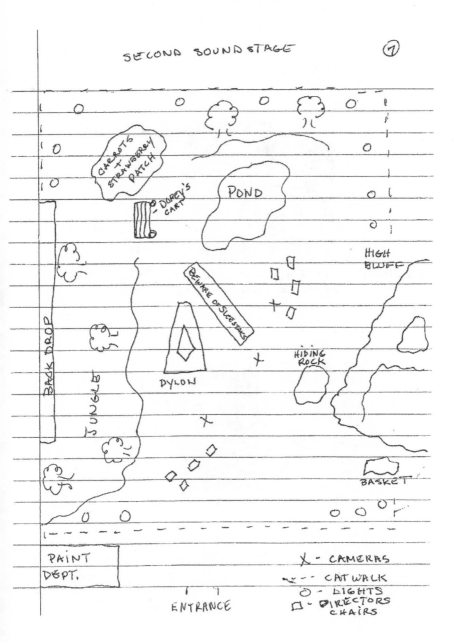

SECOND SOUND STAGE ⑦

CARROTS + STRAWBERRY PATCH

DOREY'S CART

POND

HIGH BLUFF

BACK DROP

BEWARE OF SLICESTAKS

JUNGLE

DYLON

HIDING ROCK

BASKET

PAINT DEPT.

ENTRANCE

X - CAMERAS
~ - - CATWALK
O - LIGHTS
□ - DIRECTORS CHAIRS

239

Photos

Early Brat Pack—L to R bottom: Phil Paley, Robbie Rist, Brad Savage
L to R top: Me, DeeDee Drier, Susan Olsen

Closed Set! No visitors! Colleen and I

Photos

Post *Land of the Lost* publicity pics

Photos

With SUPERMAN's Jimmy Olsen, Marc McClure,
at Magic Mountain for the rollercoaster commercial

On location with Mark Harmon and Kent McCord on *ADAM-12*

Photos

With teen heartthrob Leif Garrett

With *Eight Is Enough* star Adam Rich

Photos

Christopher Michael Bell and Alphonzo Robert Bell

Early family photo

Photos

Trying a new look

Damaged in many ways, but still a beautiful soul

Photos

Tony and I early 90s

Photos

With my Mark

Photos

Old friends! A recent photo with Wesley and Phil

Photos

Thank you for reading.

ACKNOWLEDGEMENTS

LIST OF ANGELS
(in no particular order)

Colleen "My Right Arm" Buck-Comanse
Mum-Marion Dorothy Coleman
Alphonzo and Marian Bell
Mark "Forever" McNulty
Victoria (True Angel)
Erica Hagen
Walker Edmiston
Regina Apple
Sue & Jim Turntine
Dr. Joe Willardsen
Tim Bendig
Carol Cling
Bob Swain
Shawn O'Donnell
Geoie "Peepaw" Ross
Don Frankel
Troy Kinunen
Tyrone Tann
John "Bulk" Redecki
David Wacks (R.I.P.)
Tracy Erickson Bilchek
Mark F. Berry
Ted Nichelson
Peke-A-Boo Jones

SPECIAL THANKS

Steven would like to thank Rene King Thompson, Derek Tague,
Richard May, Colleen Buck-Comanse, Craig Yoe, Dee Highfield
and, of course, Kathleen, for their assistance and patience in the
preparation of this book.